Our Journey:

THE APOSTLE AND I

Yvonne Nelson, Ed.D.

Words N Wisdom Publishing
BELTSVILLE, MD

Yvonne Nelson/Words N Wisdom Publishing
Vonnel522@aol.com

Ordering Information:
Quantity sales. Special discounts are available on quantity pur-
chases by corporations, associations, and others. For details, contact the "Special Sales Department" at the email address above.

Our Journey: The Apostle and I / Yvonne Nelson. —1st ed.
ISBN 9798838383105

Contents

This book is dedicated to the memory and legacy of the man I married, my husband, the late Chief Apostle Floyd. E. Nelson, Sr. A man of great faith and notable distinction. Our shared journey was incredible and too enormous to encapsulate in these pages. A man of courage and phenomenal wisdom, strength, and knowledge. He was an Apostle called by God and fulfilled his calling, wearing the Apostle's Mantle with humility and grace. The things he taught our family and me will live on throughout ceaseless ages. I will always love him and cherish his love for me. I thank God for our life together, the children we shared, and his memory today, tomorrow, and a lifetime.

[1]

Saying Goodbye

I WAKE FROM A SLEEPLESS NIGHT in one of the most luxurious hotels - the Ritz Carlton. But I cannot appreciate the luxury and comfort surrounding me because of my heavy heart. For the first time in my life, I wake up knowing that this day will bring closure to an era in my life. It's April 13, 2019, a beautiful spring-like Saturday morning, and it's the day I will bury my husband of over fifty years. I swung my legs over the bedside and readied myself for the most challenging life task— saying goodbye. Once I'm dressed and finished packing my things, I make my way to the restaurant on the hotel's entry-level. I didn't feel like eating, but I thought I must put a little something in my stomach for physical strength. After reaching the restaurant's lobby, I was greeted by many familiar faces. Faces that have degrees of sadness and understanding and faces that show comfort. I allow myself to be embraced as I take in their outpouring of love and strength. The rest of the family arrives too soon, and it's time to make our way to the church.

1

Outside, the bright sun shines as the rows of cars stop just before us. I am ushered inside the limo while thinking about all things Floyd Sr. and the years we spent together. There were good times and not-so-good times. We made it through times of sickness and suffering, joys and sadness. Sunshine and rain.

The memories continue to flood, and I enter a state of disbelief- this can't be happening! I thought to myself, we're not going to create any more memories together! Just the idea of it made my heartache. As the morning progressed and we navigated traffic through the DMV. Our processional was in grand style as cars stopped and made way for our motorcade to pass through. I am sure the onlookers wanted to know who was being escorted. Maybe they thought it was some White House dignitary or famous individual? Little did they know we were on our way to eulogize my husband, the Chief Apostle Floyd E. Nelson, Sr. He was being honored in death, just as he was in life.

After what seemed to be miles on the roads, we finally made it to our destination, and a grand church, the City of Jericho, rose into view. The parking lot was full of cars and those who'd come to honor the life and legacy of my beloved. Adjutants and assistants lined the church entrance waiting to assist us inside. My arm is carefully but firmly grabbed, and I am gently pulled from the car. As I stood and looked up to the front entrance, my mind froze, and disbelief held me momentarily immobile. Everything began to feel unreal, and my mind spun crazily for a moment. This was not happening! I'm going to wake up soon!

But it was real, and it was happening, and sadly I was fully awake. My arm felt a slight tug, and I was being ushered forward. We paused in the foyer so the family could line up for the processional, and there lying at an angle, was the lid to my husband's casket- mahogany wood, highly polished and elegant. The embossed engraving of his name screamed out to me while bodies positioned themselves around me. I was paired with my brother-in-law, gripped his arm tightly, and steered into the sanctuary. Inside, it was a wall to wall with people. Bishops, Pastors, notable preachers, evangelists, singers, colleagues, associates, and people from every walk of life had gathered to say good-bye.

Not to mention the hundreds of souls whose life was impacted by the ministry and the friendship of my Floyd. Many of those familiar faces were filled with sadness offering me comfort through their gaze. Some looked at me with curiosity, wanting to know how I was responding to what was happening. Despite that, I continued to look around when my eyes landed on the casket positioned at the front of the church. The timing collided with our cue to walk forward, and I gripped my brother-in-law's arm tighter. The closer we moved toward the coffin, the more I couldn't tear my eyes away. It was placed vertically with the head of the casket facing the altar and the feet toward the congregation. When I looked at him, it didn't look like him. I tried to see his kind and smiling face there, but I couldn't. This wasn't him, I thought. But in my heart, I knew it was him. Of course, he looked different. He had suffered a long illness. He had lost almost all his hair and lost so much bodyweight. But this was the remains of a man who died in the faith. This was the remains of a man who fought the good fight of faith. This was a man's body, one of God's chosen vessels. It didn't look like him, but it was him. My eyes fell to his feet, and they were encased in red velvet shoes, very appropriate for this caliber of a man.

I quickly thought, "he'd have no problem dancing in those." The "Dancing Bishop" is what they affectionately called him because those feet would move to give God good praise at any time. If you've seen him dance, you know his feet had a way of gliding across the floor effortlessly. And it didn't matter what was going on during a church service- even amid his preaching; he'd stop and give God an intricate foot stomp. Many young men tried to emulate and imitate him to no avail. His dance was so unique that it was named 'The Nelson.' I like this name. The name is entirely appropriate and befitting for this Great Man of God.

Furthermore, he had earned the right to have his dance named in honor of him. No one could dance like my husband. He was often imitated but never duplicated. He danced under the unction of the Holy Spirit, and God choreographed the moves.

Finally, we stop at the body of my beloved, and my eyes drink in the rest of him. He's dressed in his official garments, the vestments of a Chief Apostle. The colors were red, white, and off-white, with cords of gold throughout. He also wore the high hat, the Miter, the gold cross, and the apostle's gold and ruby ring. Tears seep down my face as I hold onto the arm underneath me for strength to stay standing. I signal to Apostle's brother that I'm ready to take my seat, and I wait as they say their tearful goodbye. Once the whole family was seated, the service began, and the sound of the musical choir filled the room. Quiet sniffles could also be heard. The service was beautiful from beginning to end. Every tribute, prayer, solo, and reflection was done with style, and I will be forever grateful to the men and women who made that moment memorable. I was supposed to share words, but my grief made it challenging to speak the words I'd penned. Instead, I opted for a soft thank you. And I was most proud of our son, Bishop Floyd E. Nelson Jr., who delivered his father's eulogy. As he stood there in his regalia, I am sure he was suffering myriad emotions, but only excellence shined through. Floyd Jr. summoned the courage to remind us of the beautiful life his father had led from his childhood!

With the eulogy concluded, we had reached the moment of our final goodbye. However, I was presented with my husband's memorabilia just before the casket was closed. First, I was given the Apostle's official ring— one he'd especially designed. It was solid gold with a sizeable square-inch ruby surrounded by diamonds. Then his Cartier watch made of solid gold, marble-faced with a cluster of sparkling diamonds inlaid in the center of the marble, was pressed into my hand. The Miter, or ceremonial hat, was removed from his head and laid gently into my hands. I was with Apostle when he received these things, so it was genuinely sentimental and appropriate to accept them in remembrance of him.

As I clutched these cherished items, I thought, this is it. A chapter has ended, and the book has been closed. Now, I walk alone with only memories. But God has been with me every step of the way. I have been told I still have work to do, so I press on. I press on with the assurance that God promised never to leave me alone.

The closing of the brier was a ceremony within itself. The lid, which had been placed in the foyer, was carried into the church by six adjutants who raised it high overhead as they walked to the front of the church with slow precision. Once they were at the altar, they slowly lowered it until it was securely in place. As the pallbearers departed from the sanctuary, the body was lifted high overhead as they walked toward the exit.

The benediction followed, and slowly I stood, holding onto the ever-present arm of my brother-in-law. As we processed out, I walked gently behind the casket, and for some reason, we stopped. It was during that pause that I clutched my extra support harder. And I gave my dear husband, my leader, my friend, my Bishop, my confidant, my life partner, the man I loved for his integrity, faith, longevity, loyalty, servanthood, his love for humanity, his love for God, and his love for me: One final salute. What a man, what a legacy, and what a life well-lived.

What a life we lived.

This is Our Journey, "The Apostle and I."

[2]

Let's Begin at the Beginning

AS A YOUNG LADY, I prayed I would meet and marry the man of my dreams. The man that God had been preparing me for. I observed many couples during my waiting season; they seemed to have a beautiful life together. I dated other young men and was engaged with the ring on my finger, but we eventually grew apart after moving away to attend my nursing studies. His religious affiliation collided with my beliefs, and I knew, in the long run, it wouldn't work. He was a nice, kind young man, but he was not the one God had designed for me. My future husband was born in Muskegon, Michigan. He was born on May 1, 1937. Floyd Edward Nelson was raised primarily by his mother and was one of seven children— six boys and one girl. Before Floyd was born, while he was still in utero, his mom received a prophecy that the child she carried would be a preacher. After Floyd was born, there was no mention of the prophecy ever again because his mother did not want to influence him. But at age five, the prophecy would find its way to being fulfilled. My husband was allowed to preach, and many came out of curiosity. What was this childhood preacher gonna say? The people were astonished. His first sermon topic was, "Life comes through death."

It was almost impossible for Floyd not to become the world-renown preacher that he was. Countless Pastors and Bishops have been born into this notable family. His apostolic heritage dates back six generations. His mother worked at a furniture store to make ends meet while taking on the position of a church pianist. Before her, his grandmother, Estelle Lynn, was a faithful Mother in the church who had the Spirit of discernment and could read you like a book. She was a Spiritual Mid-Wife. She was there when hundreds of souls received the Holy Spirit in the church she attended. She was an intelligent lady, full of wisdom and knowledge. At Mother Lynn's homegoing service, the pastor asked for those who had received the Holy Spirit with her praying for them to stand. Unbelievable, over half the congregation stood up in this large church. She was an amazing, lovable Mother in Zion. Floyd's Great Grand Mother was another sweetly saved Mother in Zion. Mother Thurman. I learned that she prophesied her transition. In her testimony, during evening worship, she told the church congregation, "I'm going home tonight." She said it over and over as she praised the Lord. She went home and passed away that night. And it was Mother Thurman who was a part of the Azusa Street Revival that started under the leadership of William Seymour. The revival occurred in Los Angeles, California, from 1906 until 1915.

His extraordinariness did not stop with his preaching ability. When Floyd was eighteen, he was hired at a factory. The machine he was operating malfunctioned unexpectedly, and his arm was caught in the mechanism. He yelled for help, but no one could hear him. Eventually, the machine did an automatic shut-off, releasing his arm. He was given immediate care, and he was taken to the hospital. Emergency surgery was the order. Amputation was the recommendation. Consent had to be provided by his mom, and she refused. She prayed for him, anointed him with oil, and trusted God for healing. His prognosis was he would be paralyzed in that limb, so amputate. His mother said, "He will not be the first man who has lost the use of one limb; I'm going to trust God. No surgery, no amputation." And Floyd did not let that minor setback stop him. He continued to do everything he did before the paralysis. He even directed the choir. Amazing! Unbelievable! He clapped with one hand and played the organ with one hand. Everything he did with two hands before; he now did with one. Floyd was taught to have faith in God from his childhood. And believe me, he had extraordinary faith throughout his lifetime—crazy faith. One Sunday morning during morning worship, the service was extraordinarily high. Floyd was there praising God with the rest of the congregation. Bishop P. L. Scott, a highly anointed man, called young Floyd to the altar. He asked him if he wanted the Lord to heal him.

Floyd answered yes. He anointed him, told him to lift his normal hand, and while he was praying, God worked a miracle. Both hands were up. The un-affected hand and the paralyzed hand. Both hands were clapping. Floyd was dancing. God healed him of paralysis. What a mighty God we serve. The irony is that, while he had lost the use of his right side, he taught himself to use his left side. He became ambidextrous. He had full use of both hands. What he did with his right hand, he could do with his left hand and vice versa.

Along with his keyboard ability, Floyd was a renowned drummer. He played the drums with skill and expertise. His home church recorded a record album, and he had the privilege of being the drummer. The album hit the charts and soared to platinum on the charts, which was outstanding in those days. If you ever can find the album, listed in the credits is "Drummer, Floyd Nelson." He was sought after by many churches to accompany their choir. Occasionally, he would sit at the drums to brush up on his craft. He attended culinary school and became a Certified Chef. His cooking skills were second to none. Not only did his meals look appetizing, but they also tasted delicious. He loved to cater and, sometimes, he did a fantastic catering job here and there. Whether he cooked gourmet or soul food, it was delicious. His college education earned him degrees in Divinity and Psychology. It was during this time that he met his life-long friend and partner. We got married, and our journey began.

I learned many things as a young believer through my connection to him. At the start of our union, I was a believer, but not filled, but still seeking. That was my heart's desire. After my husband told me that there was a call on his life to start his church, I knew deep down within myself that I needed to be not just a believer only but also baptized and filled. I continued to seek the Lord for the infilling of the Holy Ghost. I had started to work on my first job as a nurse. I had accumulated a week's vacation that I must take or lose altogether. We had no plans to go anywhere; I had nothing to do. I had the time, so why not? I had an idea, and it sounded like a great idea. But first, I had to ask my husband. I was confident that this was the thing for me to do. So, timidly, I asked my husband what he thought about me going to his grandmother to tarry with. He consented, but I went to the noonday prayer at the church where his pastor was. And the mothers of the church prayed with me to seek the Holy Spirit. I prayed, tarried, and...the Holy Ghost fell on me. The Heavens opened, and God's power-filled every part of that space. And as I felt that power, I began to speak with tongues. I heard myself speak in a language I had not spoken before. I felt different; I looked different; I acted differently. After I got home, there was still that feeling of a great cleansing of my soul. This feeling lasted for several hours.

But soon, I was a doubter of what God had done. The enemy told me repeatedly that I had not been filled, and I started believing him. Maybe the mothers in the church said nothing to me that I was filled with the Holy Ghost.

But, deep within me, that still small voice told me, I already filled you. But why didn't the mothers confirm my filling to me? Why didn't they tell me? That's when I decided to go to my husband's grandmother. I was still seeking and longing for the Lord on my last vacation day. I was to return to work on Monday, so I anxiously called Mother Estell Lynn and explained my circumstance; she quietly listened and prayed. Later, I was in her home, calling on the Lord as never before to manifest Himself to me. He did. Within seconds, I spoke with tongues, praising God for His miraculous power and manifestation. I got my confirmation, and his grandmother, Mother Lynn, was a witness. I learned that those praying for you did not tell you whether or not you received the Holy Spirit. Don't let anyone tell you that you received the Holy Spirit; you must know for yourself. Yes, you need confirmation but know it for yourself. You can't go by your feelings or expressions; the evidence is speaking with other tongues.

Floyd taught me how to have faith in God through our long-lasting marriage. When my faith became weak, I rode along on his faith. I believed along with him if he was crazy enough to have supernatural belief and unwavering trust.

Not only was his faith contagious, but he was a father figure to those who had no father. Through him, my ability to nature and become a Spiritual Mother bloomed. We opened our home to give other children a place to live. Floyd and I were foster parents in California to approximately fifteen teenage children. We were also surrogate parents to a few relatives' children. Some appreciated their new home, while others didn't care. It was a challenge to do this responsibility year after year, but we did it with the help of the Lord. I am glad we accepted the challenge because some of them kept in touch, still in the church, and called us Mom and Dad.

With all the good in being married, marriage is not for the faint of heart, especially if your husband is called to minister. If you are a young lady or a lady of any age and want to accept the call of Wifehood, please get all the equipping you need to do the job: Be filled with the Holy Ghost and establish a solid personal relationship with God. You will need it. You may be able to function for a little while without it, but eventually, the rubber will meet the road.

[3]

Yvonne, the City girl

KANSAS CITY, MISSOURI, is where my journey began. Kansas City is World-famous for its contribution to Blues and Jazz styled music. Many well-known singers and musicians call Kansan City home. I was born during the worst economic downturn in the history of the industrialized world. It lasted for many years—the fifth of five children, three girls, and two boys. I was considered and called the Baby. Being looked upon as "the Baby" was a term that I didn't particularly care for because it told me, "You're not old enough; you're still a baby.

I wanted to grow up, get an education, meet, and marry the man of my dreams, have a home and children, and prosper. And all that goes with it. I believed the man of my dreams would be someone like my dad. My father was a hard-working man. I can't remember a time when he did not go to work. While we didn't have the best of everything, we made it work. We wore hand-me-downs but so did other families in the neighborhood. We always had food on the table and a roof over our heads. He also planted a garden every year but never insisted that his girls do anything in the garden. That was fine because I didn't and still don't like doing all it takes to harvest a beautiful garden. I like eating vegetables and fruit, which are delicious when cooked properly. But that's it. That's as far as I can go.

My mother and father separated and divorced when I was ten, and my father raised all five siblings. He was a devout Christian and had been in the Baptist church from his youth. Appointed to the board of deacons as a young man, he served there faithfully for the rest of his life, in the same church, for sixty-plus years. There was no question about it, Deacon Herbert E. Williams and his five children were all seen in church every Sunday, and at any time, something was going on throughout the week. Here, I developed a special love for the church and God.

My siblings started leaving home one by one. When my sister Pearl, the fourth sibling, got married, I was so happy for her. When her first baby was born, I was delighted; I took a picture of the baby to school to show my teachers and classmates. They were happy with me, or at least they pretended very well. After a while, I was home alone with nothing but my church and youth activities to keep me occupied. An uncle invited me to spend the summer in Oklahoma, in a small town called, Okay. What an unusual name, I thought. The city of Okay was mainly made up of the family. My family, lots of families. My father had brothers, his mother, uncles, nieces, nephews, and cousins in Okay. There were no girls among my father's siblings; all boys. It was like a family reunion for me. The elementary school in Okay was named after my grandfather. Fonville Elementary is the name of the school. Fonville was my grandfather.

I didn't know my grandfather, but he must have been a distinguished man to have an elementary school named after him. I had a great time there and learned so much about country living. I even tried to learn how to swim. I never got good at it because of my fear of deep water. Living in the country was rough. It was not what I was used to having or doing. Rural living has no luxury. We take things for granted that are not available unless your family has lots of money. But, because I had my cousins and friends there, the conveniences didn't matter much.

We did what we did together. I had such a great time that I didn't want to return home. My father agreed to let me stay there for my junior year in high school. For the town of Okay, our school district in Oklahoma was ten miles away, so we had to ride the school bus. For me, that was great. It was my first time riding a school bus. I thought this was cool. The high school was different and a lot smaller. My classmates were different; the teachers were different. Everything was different. Of course, it was different because I was a city girl now living in the country. I excelled there. I was smarter than my classmates and remained on the Honor Roll. They were fascinated by how I spoke the King's English without the southern drawl. I made a lot of friends there; I was popular there. I went to the Senior Prom there.

Naturally, I wanted to stay there for my senior year and

graduate there. My father said, 'No' it's time to come home. I returned home to attend my senior year of high school and graduate in Kansas City. By this time, my father was remarried, and I came home to a new house and a new woman in a new home with new rules. My stepmom was cordial to me, but we were not close. She was a Beautician, a graduate of the famous Madam C. J Walker school of Cosmetology. This was a black-owned business, and it was rare in the 50s to own a successful and renowned establishment such as this. Incidentally, the school owner introduced the first products specifically made to be used on black hair. When my stepmom styled my hair, she always made my hair look pretty. It was not until later years that we became closer. As I approached my senior year of high school, I had mastered all my classes and graduated with honors. College was on the agenda, but I had to postpone getting into college to get my degree because of adequate money for tuition, student loans, and a scholarship. Student loans had not been invented.

The next day after graduation, I left for St. Louis, MO, to live with my mother. When my parents were separated, my mother kept in close contact with us. She would often provide the extra frills we wanted and needed. I had to say goodbye to the people I loved: family, friends, classmates, and my church. St. Louis, MO., was the largest principal city in Missouri. It's the home of the world-famous Gateway Arch built on the Mississippi River waterfront in the 60s that commemorates the Lewis Clark expedition. Because St. Louis was more populated, there were more opportunities, churches, and schools. I worked and saved money to care for myself and prepare for my future. My mother tried to get me into nursing school, but it didn't work out the first time. She knew I desired to be a nurse after being hospitalized for two weeks as a child. I was incredibly impressed after seeing the nurses going about their daily routine. I imagined that one day, I would be doing these things. I could see myself walking up and down the hospital corridors, taking care of patients, giving medications, and helping them get well. I knew that I could do it. I thought that if there was some way I could magically become a nurse and skip over all the preparatory processes, I could do it. Not so. I had to continue to work until the right time to apply again.

After my father let me stay in Okay for my junior year, I attended a vocational high school in Kansas City, where I majored in Dressmaking and Designer Tailoring. I was taught all the trade tricks, what made a garment look tacky, and what made it look professional. A handcrafted garment should look store-bought from an expensive boutique when worn and not put together by an amateur. But sitting at a sewing machine all day can be a strenuous job, and I knew that was not what I wanted. Dressmaking would offer me a job, but I wanted a career. And at that time, a career in the sewing industry had a future of working in a factory or being self-employed making garments for other people., but I didn't want to sit at a sewing machine all day. So, when I finally graduated, I worked in a research laboratory in a hospital, and there I met a young man interested in me romantically. However, he didn't just have a romantic interest but was genuinely concerned about my well-being and future. He was in medical school to become a doctor. The young man was Caucasian, and society was not ready for mixed races yet; it was rare, although a few mixed couples were scattered here and there. He came from an affluent family. His father was a prominent doctor with an extensive medical practice. I knew they would not accept me as his girlfriend or wife, but we remained friends.

As we worked together, he learned that I wanted to get my degree in nursing but could not do so because of funds. He took it upon himself and sought a scholarship and grant for me to attend school. He knew where the money was and how to apply for it, and he got it done. He did all the work because he wanted to get the finances for me to have a better education and life. He could see my qualities, intellect, potential, and desire. He believed in me. He never asked me for anything in return, and I gave him nothing. Sometimes when people are kind and want something for you, it has a price tag, but he only wanted me to succeed. He asked for nothing, and I gave him nothing. He knew, what I needed to know, and he knew how to make stuff happen. God allowed our paths to cross at that time for that purpose. He got the money for my tuition, he also got money to pay for my incidental fees, and I received a monthly stipend for my transportation and food. I will always be grateful to God and him for how he was instrumental in my life by helping me achieve my goals.

I enrolled in one of the finest, most difficult schools to get into and one of the most prestigious nursing schools in the city, St. Mary's Health Center. A vast hospital that offered all facets of college training to become a nurse. I was finally here. The Sisters of St. Mary operated the school. The Nuns were very strict, meticulous in their care and treatment of patients, and very proud of their institution. I was born into hard times, this black girl with no money, but here I am. I had enrolled in college, and it wasn't easy to get here. White people surrounded me, but it didn't matter. I was there to learn, and learn I did.

The college was rigorous, and the courses were challenging. The time I had spent working in the research lab helped me immensely. I was exposed to many medical terminologies, chemistry, biology, and verbal case presentations. When classes began, there were only two black ladies in the class, me and another lady. The other lady dropped out after about one month of assignments. I don't know why she dropped out, but it was probably too difficult for her. That left only one black student there, and that was me. Being the only black face in the class, I knew I had to do exceptionally well. And I did. To my surprise, my classmates were kind to me overall, considering that segregation was still prevalent in the nation. I studied for long hours. I traveled to Kansas City on weekends but always had my books and classroom notes. Whatever I was doing, my books were close by. I surprised my teachers and my classmates because everything I did was excellent. I graduated with honors.

I was now Yvonne Williams, R.N. During my training time, I

visited and became a member of a new church member. And almost immediately after I graduated, a man named Floyd Nelson came to the church. He was a minister and an Elder. I saw him, but he was of no interest to me. Yes, he was single, good-looking, neatly dressed, had his career going, and could sing. But there was something else about him. Was it his faith in God, his personality, his humor, his intelligence, his passion, his smile that I might be interested in?

I saw some of the ladies "making eyes" at him and attempting to get his attention. He was impressive, but I knew what I wanted; I knew what I'd asked God for in my future husband, and I had a purpose to fulfill.

But, he was not my type.

[4]

Could this be God?

FLOYD E. NELSON WAS HIS NAME; no, he was not my type. But there was something special about him. The way he carried himself. The way he smiled. The way he talked. The way he sang gave new meaning to the words of the song. Yes, there was something unusual about him. He was not like your average man on the parade, checking out the ladies to see who would be his next victim. He was different. I didn't particularly like how he dressed, but he was clean and unique in his walk, talk, and devotion.

Floyd was unlike any other man I knew.

He was polite and well-mannered. Charming even. A lovely gentleman who was a pleasure to meet in those days. I think it was his smile and his eyes for me. And to know that he was a minister made it more special.

I didn't talk to him, and he didn't speak to me. But I knew he was there; apparently, he knew I was there.

While I noticed his rareness, I was unphased. I wasn't looking for him or any man because I was there to praise the Lord. But soon, he caught my attention because he was different.

I was feeling pretty good about myself. I was a college graduate and self-sufficient. I'd recently started a new career and had bought a new car. Plus, I went to church regularly. Correction, more than the regular basis. Our church had four primary services on Sunday, including Sunday school. We had morning worship, afternoon service, radio broadcast, and night service. My girlfriends and I went to all the services. If there were something else going on in the city such as a musical or concert, which many times there was, we'd go to that service too. Church service was always good. Good preaching, good teaching, good singing, and good dancing. That's when I discovered that Floyd was an anointed praiser. His sincere praises captured the attention of the entire church. He loved to praise the Lord in the dance. All he had to do was think of the goodness of Jesus, and praise would begin. That was the main attraction for some churches next to the Word.

At one of our church services, Floyd was asked to sing. This was the first time I heard him sing. The song that he chose was "Wake Up in Glory." That's an old church song, but the words are significant. His voice moved me. The song had a good beat, and Floyd had swagger.

Here are the words:

I shall fall asleep some sweet day
And from earth shall pass away
And my soul shall reach a better land
When my weary eyelids close
And I've sunk to sweet repose
Singing hallelujah as I go

When I wake, wake, wake up in glory
And to Jesus, I'll sing redemption story
Oh, I shall see His blessed face
He who has saved me by His grace
When I wake up in glory by and by.

I said to myself, wow, this man can sing. There was something about his voice and his command of the audience. He seemed to draw them in with his smile and with his eyes.

Everybody was into his voice. It was amazing.

On one Sunday afternoon, between services, I was waiting for my car to be delivered to me after getting it washed. I waited and waited without the return of my vehicle. I was in a hurry to leave with my friends, so I asked Floyd if he would get my car and keep it for me until I returned. He politely agreed. We had never been formally introduced or interacted, but something was about this man. I believed I could trust him, and I was right.

While I was away eating dinner, my car was delivered to the hands of Floyd. When I returned to the church, Floyd returned my car keys, and I said thank you. We said good night, and we went our separate ways. But he had got my phone number from a friend unknowingly to me. His side of the story is that I made eyes at him. That's funny. Perhaps I did, but that was not my intention; I was just being nice. And that's when it all started.

The hospital where I had gone to school and trained to be a nurse offered me my first job. It was a surgical nurse position. I accepted this job for personal reasons, so I would not have to work on weekends. As a rule, no surgery was performed on the weekend except for emergencies. I would need special training, but I learned on the job, which was a stressful way to learn. This made working in the operating room extra tedious. I learned to distinguish between hundreds of surgical instruments needed for numerous procedures. I learned to anticipate what the Dr. needed with him saying nothing, just holding out his hand. I knew every instrument and its use, from the smallest to the largest. Sometimes with tears in my eyes because the surgeons were complex and not easy to work with. But I was determined to master this skill. And I did. I got good at what I was doing. The surgeons noticed my proficiency and many times would ask for my assistance. As the surgeons would walk into the O.R. and look at the giant board to see who was assisting them, you could see relief come over their faces when they saw my name.

That was a milestone accomplishment for me.

One day, the operating room seemingly had a revolving door. I was assigned case after case. I had to be sharp, alert, and instantaneous. Surgeons can be impatient and even arrogantly mean, so I had to be ready and not make any mistakes. I was tired and just wanted to go home and rest. Just as I was settled in for the evening, the phone rang. And to my surprise, it was Floyd!

I declare to you; that we talked for hours. We had just met, and I didn't know he had my phone number. My tiredness seemed to evaporate. During the conversation, he said, "Now, when we get married...." I was like, "Married? Who are you going to marry? Not me." It was just like that—just that simple. There was no proposal, no ring, and no asking. He told me I was going to be his wife.

I started looking more closely and listening attentively to what this man said. His conversation was soothing and exciting. We talked about church and the future, and we talked about us. Many days and nights, we would talk for hours. And in my house, we only had one phone. The cord was short, and there was little or no privacy. I tried to take the cord around the corner into the bathroom so we could talk, but most times, that was futile. I liked talking to him. He had a lot to say, and I had the time to listen. He spoke about his future, his career as a chef, and our future together. Eventually, love came into the picture, and I was sold.

We went out on dates when I wasn't engaged with things or when his schedule would permit. That's when I saw the quality and type of man he was. He always came to the house to pick me up. He didn't toot the car horn and wait for me to come out. He went to the front door to get me, chatted with my mother, escorted me out, and opened the car door. He wouldn't allow me to open doors; he opened them for me. He assisted me in and out of the car. Not because I needed help, but because he was a gentleman. When we were out to dinner, he always slid my chair back to allow me to sit at the table, and when it was time to leave, he did the same thing. He did all the things and more. He was a gentleman. He did this throughout our lives and continued to do them even when we got older. That's a good thing because everything slows down when you get older and need a little assistance.

After noticing our conversations went far into the night, my mother said, "you all need to hurry up and get married so we can all get some sleep."

We chuckled. I firmly believe that had my father not insisted that I come home to Kansas City, perhaps we would have never met. It is because God knew that I would eventually move to St. Louis. Had I not done that, I probably would have never met him. Even though we lived within a two-block radius of each other, we were neighbors, you might say, but our paths never crossed until they crossed in God's time.

I was smitten. And knew I wanted to be his wife by this point, but I couldn't help but wonder if...... was he to be my husband? Was I destined to be his wife?

As a young lady, I wanted to marry a minister. I thought the minister was close to God and wanted to be close to God.

Despite all those inner doubts and my many misgivings and uncertainties, we began to plan our wedding. I was a little doubtful because I had only known him for a short time: six weeks. So, I didn't know much about him. Doing a background check or a credit check was unheard of. Most of his family was miles away-- I couldn't ask them. The most important thing to me was that I didn't want to make a mistake. I knew that God worked in mysterious ways; His ways are not our ways, nor His thoughts our thoughts. I also knew that destiny has a way of getting things to come to pass by God's divine order, void of our understanding. But I was still nervous. As I continued to pray about the situation and seek God's guidance, I couldn't help but wonder if this was my destiny and my answered prayer.

Could this be God?

[5]

The steps In-Between

MOST YOUNG GIRLS DREAM of becoming beautiful brides and intelligent and influential ladies. My life was no different. I dreamed of one day marrying a Minister. At the time, I didn't know what I wished for, and I had no idea of the life I was dreaming about. At the church I attended in St. Louis, my Pastor and his wife enamored me. They were role models for me. I liked the way he preached and broke down the Word. He had charisma. I was fascinated by my pastor's wife. She was beautiful, had poise, and was very talented. She had a way of loving the young ladies and took time with us. She was a great hostess when she invited us to their home and was a gracious lady in the church. She would often sing lead in the choir or sing a solo before the pastor preached. I could see myself walking in her shoes.

Most importantly, they openly expressed their love for each other subtly and cutely.

I think that is very critical for couples in ministry to do. It can keep others from interfering with the marriage vows when they know the love you share for each other. It leaves little room for infidelity and unfaithfulness unless the outsider is crazy.

Now, the Lord heard my request and gave me the desires of my heart.

While we were both still at our former church where we met and had gotten engaged, a dear mature woman evangelist in the church came to me in a sincere voice and told me not to marry him. Her reasons were vague and unsubstantiated. She didn't want me to be hurt, she says. This was the same lady who I later learned had repeatedly insisted that her husband and his secretary go places together without her. I talk about this in another chapter. I went to our Pastor and told him what had been said to me. He didn't show concern but instead gave us his blessing. That's all we needed, and the wedding was on.

As I think back, as much as I wanted to be a Pastor's wife, there may have been times when I thought I was crazy to want such a thing. Why couldn't I desire an ordinary man with regular working hours, like a nine to five position? Or someone who could always give uninterrupted time to his family. A man who wouldn't be thronged by many people waiting to see him at all odd hours of the day and night with their problems and emergencies. There would be no disgruntled Deacons or frustrated Church members telling him what he could or could not do.

I wasn't as prepared for that part of life, but Floyd was. He told me before we married that God was first in his life. He meant that. He dearly loved me; he said so many times. He showed me in many ways that he loved me. Nothing was too good, costly, or extravagant for me, but God was first. If he had to stay at the church working into the wee hours of the morning, putting his carpentry skills into action, getting God's house ready for worship, that's what he did because he wanted God's house to be beautiful. He often worked alone because his helpers had other things to attend to. I must say, when he laid his tools down, we had a beautiful place to worship. It was not the cathedral, but it was beautiful. I had to accept that as part and parcel if I was going to marry him.

There was a little respite, however.

Before Apostle Nelson was called to pastor, a sister in the church told me that if she had a husband that could preach like him, she would be praying for the Lord to give him a church. I told her I was in no hurry because I enjoyed having him to myself, but the day finally came for him to step out on his own. He wasn't waiting for a Pastor to die or a pulpit to become vacant. He waited on the Lord for directions. He stepped out on faith with the pastor's blessings when the time was right.

I didn't realize it at the time, but when I look back, I can see where the Lord was preparing me to be a Pastors wife. In the church I grew up in, we learned to do everything. Of course, one of the first things we learned was we sang with the children's choir, 'The Sun Beams.' Then we sang in the Jr. choir and eventually the senior choir, and we served on the Jr. Usher board. In the choir, I was one of the principal lead singers. We also were members of the Jr. Missionaries and learned how to be benevolent to those in need. I even taught the children's Sunday school class as a teen. The BY-PU (Baptist Young Peoples Union) or BTU (Baptist Training Union) were a must to attend.

That's where we got our training to work in other areas of the church.

They taught us how to do everything about the church duties, such as: How to preside over a meeting using Robert's Rules of Order; How to record minutes; how to offer a motion, entertain and carry a motion; how to keep accurate financial records; and all other aspects of church operations. The young men were taught to be a Deacon, and the young ladies were taught to be a Hostess and missionaries. We learned all these things and more while learning about the Lord. I first learned to love the Lord in this church and wanted to walk closer to Him.

And after Floyd found a suitable building, we were off and running. The building was a storefront with living quarters upstairs and a full basement. We moved in. Pastor Nelson hammered and nailed to transform the storefront into a suitable place of worship. In this first church, we both discovered things about each other. I found that he had carpenter skills, and Pastor Nelson discovered that I could play the organ a little bit, and I played until we could get a skilled musician. People began to come, some from our previous church and others from other churches, and many who were unchurched came. There I was, a Pastors wife, a First Lady, and a Mother in the church, even though I was a young woman. At 33 years of age, they began to call me Mother. I played the organ, sang, ushered, taught Sunday school, Sunday school superintendent, Missionary, cook, shopper, housekeeper, bus driver, and Women's President, Financial secretary. I did it all. I filled in and did whatever was needed until the Lord blessed us with other willing workers. And He did.

Our church grew fast. We baptized many souls in the Name of Jesus. Not only that, but we acquired a radio broadcast and broadcast once a week. We were heard by hundreds, perhaps thousands of people, potential souls that would be saved. Another dear lady and I was the radio announcer with no prior experience, but we did it to the glory of God.

While living in St Louis, we were blessed to purchase two large churches simultaneously. One church in St Louis is now a historic landmark, the Black Reparatory Theater. The other church is in Mt. Vernon, Illinois. Approximately 70 miles away. Seventy miles separated the churches from each other. Floyd was already a Pastor in St. Louis and was appointed Pastor in Mt. Vernon. Day after day, week after week, month after month, and year after year, we journeyed between the two churches, preaching and teaching. Amid Floyd working so hard, he had a mild heart attack. That's when he knew he should slow down. This was not only difficult for this young, energetic pastor but also his family. But we did this until he got further instructions from God.

Eventually, my husband was led to move on. The church was left in the hands of his Assistant Pastor.

Floyd followed the leading of the Lord, and he knew it was time to move on. We moved to the next assignment, San Diego, California, which was very familiar because we had been there several times. San Diego is a beautiful city located on the coast of California. It is situated at the foot of mountains and desert and expands alongside the Pacific Ocean. It is picturesque with gorgeous, beautiful beaches where the waters are warm and a beautiful sky-blue, and the sunsets breathtaking. It was not unheard of for people to go hiking or camping in the mountains and swim in the ocean on the same day. San Diego is a military town and home to thousands of military personnel. It has several large Naval, Coast Guard, National Guard, and Marine Corps Bases in surrounding areas. When these young men and women and their families visited our church, they made their church home with us.

Apostle was a skilled swimmer and learned to swim in the waters of Lake Michigan. Being hydrophobic, I never learned how to swim. Although we were not avid beach fanatics, Apostle sometimes went to the beach to enjoy watching the ebb and flow of the tide and read and pray. I believe some of his best messages were birthed on the shores of San Diego.

We knew many pastors there because the Apostle had

probably preached in every Apostolic church in the city. Many souls were saved, and churches grew during his revivals. When these churches learned of his move to the city to start a church, some vowed to close every door that was once opened to him. And that's what they tried to do. We were told that San Diego is a "preacher's graveyard." This meant that trying to build a church there would kill you. And it was tough there, but the hand of God was on his life. Despite the many doors being closed to him, Pastors of other denominations were drawn to his ministry and called on him for advice and leadership. His popularity grew, even expanding through the United States and beyond.

My husband was a builder and founder of churches, somewhat like the Apostle Paul, who established many churches. If needed, he would set things in order and install a pastor. As soon as we could build up a church with a sizable membership and it was financially stable, the Lord would impress on him to move on. It was heartbreaking to leave people I lived and labored in the gospel with him, but I had no say in the matter. Where he went, I went.

Difficult? Yes! Heartbreaking, yes. With each move we made, it became harder and harder. Even though he always put the churches in capable hands when we left, these were our babies and children; we prayed for them, taught them, baptized them, and worked with them. We were like family, even to this day. To say that it is heartbreaking is putting it mildly.

We also had to consider that moving out of state meant

new schools for the children. They had to leave their best friends, schools, classmates, church members, and people dear to them. I must say they adapted quickly and made new friends and classmates easily.

In San Diego, I was appointed as Chaplain of the Women's Correctional Facility, the women's jail. I ministered to hundreds of women locked up and serving time for murder. There were also crimes of robbery, thievery, drug abusers, drug dealers, domestic violence and abuse, and parole violations. I was not afraid to do my assignment because I knew that I could be the only individual who would lead them to Christ. These women needed someone they could talk to and someone who would listen. Compassion is a gift that is not seen often among churchgoers. People want revenge and punishment for crimes committed. That's true, but compassion is also in order when applied appropriately. I looked forward to the days I would go to the facility to minister; it was rewarding.

Also, in San Diego, while I was working in a Drs. Office, a lady came in and offered me a teaching position at a local college. I had no teaching experience to speak of other than teaching Sunday school. I talked to Apostle Nelson about it, and he said, if you want it, it's yours. The college administrators accepted my application, resume, experience, and inexperience. They hired me to teach Medical Assistants and Certified Nursing Assistants. Two different colleges., two different courses. In the classroom, I was very strict. I wanted my students to be the best, most committed nurses in the field. I took my position seriously and insisted that they do the same. I was strict, but I was fair. I didn't give them a grade that they didn't deserve. Some of the best nursing personnel passed through my instructions because God used me as a no-nonsense teacher who loved what she did. I not only cared about getting the job done, I cared about the person and their problem with empathy, and I tried to instill that same standard of care in my students. It was not until I left those positions that I obtained the necessary credentials that qualified me to teach a college course in the state of California. I did this for about eight years, and it was a big financial blessing for us and opened doors for us in the work of the ministry.

I felt like a military wife moving when her husband received new orders. Everything familiar to her she had to leave behind and embark on new and different surroundings. Floyd says that there were about thirty churches or more that he established. I lost count. All I know is it was a whole lot of churches.

Our last move was from San Diego, California, to Maryland. And leaving the West Coast to go to the East Coast... people thought we were crazy to leave a beautifully warm climate behind and embrace a cold, freezing environment with ice and snow. San Diego weather was like summertime, almost year-round. Some mornings were gloomy looking, but later, the sun would shine, and it was a beautiful day. It only rained during the rainy season, which lasted a few days—no ice, snow, hurricanes, tornados, and almost perfect weather every day. There may be an occasional earthquake, but they were few and far between. The East Coast, however, has four seasons. From ice and snow to blue skies and sunshine, a bit of this and a lot of that.

And although moving was not easy because, with each move, you leave people behind, you leave some part of yourself and your attachments behind. One time during a move, our wedding pictures were accidentally left behind. We didn't realize it until several weeks passed, and it was too late to track them down. That was before the days of computer technology and storage space in the clouds. However, I never debated with him about leaving an established church.

Floyd insisted I leave my job and be a homemaker. I did and used some of my free time to attend Bible college. Most of the students were of other denominal persuasions. But, I wasn't there to debate religion with anyone; I was there to learn. I loved being back in school, and I was a model student. After completing all required subjects, testing, and writing my dissertation, I was awarded a Doctoral Degree in Christian Education. (Ed. D) I was so elated.

Yes, I often thought he was out of his mind and a bit cray-cray, but I didn't want to interfere with the work of the Lord. I wondered, how can you put in all this labor, blood, sweat, and tears and turn and walk away. But, it was not for me to know an Apostle's inter-workings. Being an Apostle is a calling, a high calling, and it's not always an easy or glamorous life. And although I didn't know it initially, it was what I signed up for when I said: "I do."

We lived in San Diego for twenty-one years. The Lord brought us there to spread the gospel, grow, and learn more about ministry and people. The years we spent here were productive, as were all the places we lived in. Every experience was challenging but informative and beneficial. Thank God for what we learned and the bittersweet life in the sun. Nobody said the road would be easy, and He didn't bring us this far to leave us. We came this far by faith.

[6]

The trip to the Altar

LIVING IN THE SIXTIES WAS QUITE AN EXPERIENCE. Times were difficult. Most people were struggling to survive daily. People who seemed to be living a life of luxury were few and far between, and some were getting things illegally. If you wanted to have anything, you had to work hard for it and manage it well if you wanted to keep it.

I had only known him for about six weeks when the Apostle and I married. We did not need to marry so quickly because we were not expecting a baby, and he was not being sent overseas in the military, and had we chosen to wait a little longer, we could have. He didn't want me to get away, and he decided to put a ring on my finger.

I hardly had time even to plan a wedding. I barely had enough time to pick out my dress and shoes and order flowers and a cake. I hardly had any money, at least not enough to start planning a big wedding; I had just started working on my career. I was fresh out of college, still green and ignorant with stars in my eyes. Tina Turner said, "What's Love got to do with it?" A whole lot. Because our love was real and lasting.

The wedding day came on a brisk day in October. I walked down the aisle to be united in marriage for life. There was no time to send invitations, so everyone was invited. The church was packed. Every seat was taken because we got married after a Sunday morning service. Everybody wanted to see this wedding. It was on a small scale but elegant, well-designed, and stylish. I wore a beautiful turquoise dress with a matching pillbox hat, a short veil, and all the right finishing touches. I looked stunning, and Floyd looked so handsome. We exchanged our vows, and I meant every word I said; I became Mrs. Yvonne Nelson in minutes. We exchanged matching gold wedding bands that day with three small diamonds in the center. It was beautiful. Our pastor prayed over us, wished us well, gave us his blessings, and we were on our way.

The reception was held in the fellowship hall of the church. We didn't have much money, but we had a cake and other light refreshments. We kept the cake for the traditional year. We tried to eat a small bite on our first anniversary, but it wasn't enjoyable.

The first night of our honeymoon was spent in our newly acquired apartment, with no glitz, no glam. But Floyd made it all up to me later. He promised he would take me places, and we would travel and see the world, and he kept his promise.

We stayed in some of the finest 5-star hotels worldwide in later years. We have dinned in some of the most exquisite restaurants globally and have seen the world's seven wonders, save one. He bought me the finest clothes, diamonds, and furs; nothing was too good or costly for me. Like most newlyweds, it was hard for us to adjust to married life. I was used to my independence, and he was used to being the head. He would preach to me, quote scriptures and drop hints about what I should be doing. He would constantly remind me that he was the head and the man was the head of the home. I got a little flustered hearing it repeatedly. He told me, "I'm the head," and I said, 'Well, if you're the head, I'm the neck, and you can't turn without me." We both looked at each other and broke out laughing. We laughed so hard that we forgot about what we were disputing. It took me a while, but I finally settled in, and it was easier for me to understand what a strong man he was and how to be the wife he needed me to be.

I remembered that he grew up with 'old school' teachings and traditions, which I was not used to. While my name had changed from Williams to Nelson, I was the same girl: optimistic in my thoughts and dreams. Being so optimistic, I guess I wasn't prepared for the things ahead.

Please understand, young ladies, I do not recommend you do what I did. I married quickly, hardly knowing him. Take your time and get to know the person. Date them a while. Times are a lot different now. Deception lurks on the internet and dating websites. Check them out thoroughly. You may even want to do a background check. See what's in his background and by all means, check his credit. You will never know all there is to know but take your time. You learn many things once married: the good and the not-so-good. Our marriage worked out because we made it work. It paid off because we were determined to stay together. I don't regret doing what I did by marrying him so quickly because it gave me more time to spend with him. I wish I had more.

Our marriage survived for over fifty years. Yes, it wasn't easy. Yes, it was hard at times. But we took our vows seriously. That was the secret of our marital success.

Although Floyd was a provider, I knew I could contribute to the household financially by being employed. So, I continued working as a scrub and circulating nurse in the operating room. I loved what I did, but some surgeons were downright mean. They were good at what they did, but the tension and stress of cutting someone open and removing organs caused them to act as they did. Because of the harsh verbal language, I often assisted the surgeons with tears rolling down my face behind my surgical mask. But I stayed there because I was determined not to let the complication of learning this skill defeat me. I had made it up in my mind that I would be one of the best O.R. nurses in our department, this side of the Mississippi.

As I look back on things today, the things they did and said to the nurses they could not do today. It would be classified as harassment. Harassment in the workplace was unheard of or not listened to. I could have left the job and quit, but I had responsibilities, and we needed my salary at the time. But the stress and tension in my job added to the stress and anxiety of being a newlywed. I was trying to learn a skill on the job and, at the same time, learn how to be a wife. There were many things that I didn't know about our future, but every day I learned something new. I didn't know that he would quit his job as a Master Chef and become full-time in the ministry within three years. I didn't know before our wedding ceremony that there would be only one paycheck coming in, and that would be mine. I had to stretch one salary to cover all household expenses, plus food, clothing, and gas. Trying to divvy our money was an act of genius. Many bills were late or were left unpaid. Sometimes it was an oversight, and other times it was because there was insufficient money with only one actual salary.

Because of the demand for his ministry style and anointing, many Pastors wanted him to come to their churches to conduct revivals. I didn't know that he would go to those churches; one church would lead to another, and he would sometimes be away from home for a few weeks. When he came home, I thought he would at least have sufficient money, but it was never enough to cover everything. I found out later that he would leave much of his pay with the church he was with. His priority was the church. He did tell me this during one of those long conversations on the phone. However, I heard it but didn't believe it. I should have believed it. Our family made years of sacrifices for the ministry. If there is such a thing as catching up, he certainly tried to give me everything I ever wanted. I tried to keep my wants and wishes moderate and not go to extremes because he would try to do it for me.

He was an experienced, certified chef but didn't want to cook at home because he was exhausted from doing ministerial duties. I didn't bother him about cooking; I did it myself. At the beginning of our marriage, I was very intimidated about my cooking because Floyd was a certified chef. But he never complained about my cooking.

He didn't want to wear the food, so he always said the food was good.

I also learned that he was a little stubborn when it pertained to the things of God. There were a lot of things that I didn't know. I thought that he was the epitome of masculinity of the opposite sex. He was all that and a big bag of chips. He was my cup of tea, the cream in my coffee, and the butter on my toast.

Ladies, let me repeat. I wouldn't advise you to do what I did and marry after a few short weeks. Check him out for everything! Down to a health screening. Get to meet his family, especially his mother. If the man says something like, "My mom and I don't get along very well." Run! There's something wrong when a man who can't get along with his mother! A mother will go the last mile of the way for her children. When a mother severs that relationship with her child, something is wrong. I advise you to run the other way.

I didn't meet my Mother-in-law until after we were married. We drove to Michigan to her home, where the children grew up. She was genuinely lovely, loving, and a saved woman of wisdom. I liked her immediately. She was in my corner. She was someone I could talk to and someone who understood. I truly miss her.

I often thought I had made a big mistake in my marriage to this giant of a man. But something deep inside me kept telling me to stick it out.

Conversely, he found out that there were some things that he didn't know about me either, but I won't go into that. There's no need to bore you with the details about me. During those times, I am glad that I knew Jesus. I'm so happy I was saved. I'm glad I had an anchor to build my life upon.

I want to tell you that it was God who kept us together. It was God who taught me how to let Him fight my battles. God reminded me of the vows we took and the promises we made... "Till death do we part."

Before we got married, in one of our many conversations, he told me that he would take me to places that I'd never been. He said that we would never be broke again; we would live in houses built for people with lots of money. He promised me lots of things.

Today I can say he gave me all those things and more.

Stand still if you are reading this book and your marriage or circumstance is somewhat shaky. We serve a God who can turn it around. He did for me, and I know He will do it for you! Many couples are headed to divorce court because they can't solve their problems. But somewhere amid their situations, God worked it out.

Marriage is not only about the good times and the lovemaking. You have to get out of bed and handle the issues of life. Marriage is a mixture of good things and not-so-good things and knowing that things will get better. Sometimes, things worsen before they improve because your marriage is placed under a magnifying glass, and things appear enormous. But don't panic. It's only for a season. Seasons change.

What's so sad is...people make determinations about their future based on what's happening now. Don't base your future on the drama that's going on in your life right now. Your marriage might not be at its best, and everything might not be clicking on all cylinders...but take ownership that God has called you to possess it. Recognize that God wants your marriage to be clicking on all cylinders...I know your children might be giving you drama, driving you crazy, or stressing you out. But God gave you that family, and it may not seem like it's working out right now, but God has an assignment for you. It may be tough now. Challenging and stressful. But do things right, and it will start clicking.

Here's a story I remember hearing a long time ago:

There was a store called "The Husband Store," where you come to get a husband. There are different husbands on each floor...but once you go on a floor, that's the floor you must shop on. You can't come off that floor and shop at another..., and if you pass a floor going up, you can't come back down to shop on it.

The sign on the 1st floor says...all these husbands are saved, and love the Lord.

2nd floor...They are saved...love the Lord...and love their wives.

3rd floor... They are saved...love the Lord...and love their wives...and love their kids.

4th floor... They are saved...love the Lord...and love their wives...and love kids...and cooks and cleans.

5th floor... They are saved...loves the Lord...and loves their wives...and loves kids...and cooks and cleans...and is romantically inclined.

She got off. "This is the floor for me," she said. A big sign was waiting for her which read...there have been 4,847,398 women who have been here to get husbands, and there's no husband left for you. We are out of husbands. What! Out of husbands? It can't be! She continued to look further. She saw other women crying and woefully returning to the elevator because they couldn't find a husband "satisfactorily."

The moral is...He may not be perfect. He may still have some flaws; there may be many things he still has to learn. But work with him until he understands it. My advice is to keep what you've got because you don't know what you'll get. Nobody's perfect. Mr. Right does not exist. Nobody's got one hundred percent of anything. Love the things that attracted you to him. Remember, you are not perfect either.

The Lord has someone made especially for you.

[7]

The Mandate

THE DMV. Washington, DC, Maryland, and Virginia. Three locales so close together you don't know when you're leaving one and entering another without signs. If I were to compare the two places, East and West coast, California made you feel like you were in a foreign country. You could hear a foreign language spoken at any given the time of day. And after living there for several years, surrounded by other nationalities and cultures, when we relocated to the DMV, I received a culture shock! African Americans were everywhere and running everything. They were in prominent places with note-worthy careers doing extraordinary things, which made me proud to see it happening.

For me to get employment, I must reapply for state licensure. Another one of my childhood dreams was to become a teacher by this time. I had acquired my teaching credential and taught college courses to prospective nurses trying to get their degrees. I enjoyed what I was doing, which was a rewarding and stimulating aspect of my life. I did not want to go through the process, and Floyd didn't want me to go through the reapplication ordeal. He politely told me to leave the job, lay my career aside, and work with him full-time in the ministry. That's precisely what I did, and I have never worked another day. Instead, we enhanced our union as complementary partners in marriage and Christ. I was ready to give up getting up before dawn, driving on jam-packed freeways, and dealing with hard to get along with employees. I will always carry the skills I have learned in my heart and remember how God blessed me to achieve them. A doctor once told me that nurses don't retire; they stop getting paid. I agreed. But we praise God from whom all blessings flow. Although I missed a paycheck on payday, I learned to adjust, and God cared for all our needs.

When the fall season was approaching during our first year in Maryland, we both wondered where the summer went because we enjoyed the summer-like weather throughout December and beyond in California. The quick climate change took some getting used to. In California, the Bible Way Church Worldwide was our spiritual covering. Fellowship with our sister churches was seldom or only during convention times as there was only one other Bible Way church in Northern California about five hundred miles away. Moving to the east coast put us closer to other Bible Way churches where we could fellowship and visit.

Shortly after we arrived in Maryland, my husband worked with his brother, Bishop James D. Nelson, Sr., in Baltimore, MD. He assisted him in organizing a new reformation called World Assemblies of Restoration. (W.A.R.) For a year, he worked with him, planning, organizing, preaching, teaching, traveling, and building. I knew he would pastor again and prayed for the Lord to bless my husband and me with a move-in-ready church. A church where he didn't have to tear down walls, build walls and platforms so that we could have church. I thought the Lord had answered my prayers.

About a year later, when a Bible Way church became available in Washington, DC, he was called to become a pastor and was once again active in Bible Way full-time. The church was beautiful, newly renovated, and just the right size for us to grow. The membership was minimal and comprised primarily of seniors, but we seemed to grow instantaneously. The members loved Apostle Nelson.

Things didn't work out at that church, and he was only there for one year. As we were planning his installation services, the tables were turned. The Apostle was out. With one telephone call and a few unsatisfied people, He was out.

He was affectionately called a Modern Day Moses because he led the people out after being without proper leadership for years. God had a change of plans. About ninety percent of the congregation, or more, left with him.

I was in California at the time. Our daughter was giving birth, and I was needed there. I missed it all. Earlier that

Sunday morning, when I tried to contact him by phone, I got no answer. I knew something wasn't right. But the Lord allowed me to miss it all.

The night he left the church, he founded the Lively Stone Church of God, Washington, DC.

A Bible Way church.

While we were at Lively Stone, Floyd celebrated fifty years of ministry. Guest came from the four corners of the states and various locations. My oldest sister Ruth and others traveled for many miles, but she was there to witness this glorious celebration. We tried to cover every chapter of his life depicted in a video, including our journey together.

It was the event of the decade.

At the close of this affair, we were given the keys to a Mercedes Benz with a built-in navigation system, which I had wanted.

We were so excited.

He was appointed to work in areas where Bible Way needed help. Apostle Nelson was a servant. He was not there to be ministered unto but to minister.

He adopted this mindset.

He was assigned to work with other countries to reignite their growth. We traveled in the U.S and out of the country to serve wherever help was needed. We traveled to England, Africa, Jamaica, Trinidad and Tobago, Canada, South Korea, Japan, Israel, Africa, Italy, and many other countries. The Apostle enamored the people, but I was included and was the principal speaker in women's groups and the leading speaker at services on some of those occasions. I was invited to come to London several times on my own. It was then that I became internationally known. When I recorded a CD, my caption was, "Taking the Gospel to the World."

After the transition of our Diocesan, he was appointed Diocesan of the District of Columbia. Apostle Nelson and I served this Great organization faithfully. We have attended every convention for the last thirty-one years, and at this time, only missing one. We attended when money was good, and we came when money was funny. I tried my best to serve our senior mothers when I saw they needed assistance.

I would volunteer to assist, not even looking for recognition or to be paid or compensated. One year while still living in California, I was asked to give a presentation to the Clergy Wives on "Teenage Pregnancy." I gladly accepted. I had several months to prepare, so I got busy trying to collect all the data I could find on the subject. The internet was not invented yet, so I spent many hours in the public library, compiling information for my presentation. Finally, I was ready to speak to these great women. Women that I looked up to and women I wanted to be like.

When the time for the convention came, I packed my best clothes in anticipation of being among my sisters. The women in Bible Way were fashionable dressers. They knew how to put their clothes together to make an impression and a statement. I could not compete with them on this level, but I wanted to look my best. So, I packed my best clothes, shoes, and hats to make an impression. The time for the Clergy Wives session was approaching. My anxiety had been building for weeks. Finally, the day for us to travel arrived. My nervousness was probably evident as I entered the room where our session was held. I was anxious, and it may have shown on my face, I don't know, but I was ready with facts and figures. I had done my research and was prepared to talk to them with points, hand-outs, and headlines on this controversial subject.

I was feeling good about myself. Finally, I thought, someone had noticed my abilities and the capabilities in me and wanted me to expound. I was a bit nervous but excited and willing to do my best.

This was my first presentation and the first time I had been asked to speak to this group of well-known Bishops and Pastor's wives. I was ready. At last, we were in our meeting place. We shared in the opening preliminaries and necessaries of business, which lasted a long time. The hour was growing late, and we were out of time. Our time was up, and we had to adjourn just like that. Adjourn? But I hadn't given my presentation. I researched, planned, had all the facts, and had hand-outs and information, but there was no time left. I was omitted and left out, and I felt discriminated against. After all, who was I? They must think I'm just a General Board Bishop's wife, not Executive Board. Just a small fry. Yes, your husband is a Bishop. Yes, your husband can preach well. But the two of you are not upper echelon people; what does it matter if you give your presentation or not.

The group president gave me an apology and asked me if I

would make my presentation at the next meeting, and of course, I said yes. I waited for them to tell me where and when that would be, and they never did. All my research and hard work went down the drain. I was crushed.

I never told anyone about my experience. I kept it all to myself. I had to deal with the disappointment, the hurt, the embarrassment, and the feeling of being overlooked. I kept it all inside and developed a thick skin.

Thick skin is essential in our walk of faith.

If we allow it, the slightest things will upset us and make us feel like quitting. You will undoubtedly be overlooked, talked about, or even ridiculed. Inevitably, something will happen to try to get you off your course. Try not to get into your feelings. Don't take everything personally. My advice is to hang on in there. Stick-it-out. You will be better for it if you do. I was determined not to let this disappointment stop me from serving, and eventually, I got over it. I worked with the Missionaries, the Clergy Wives, and Widows, sang with the Clergy Wives Choir during the convention, and was Vice President of the Women's Council. I enjoyed it all.

Sadly, a few years after the transition of our founder, Apostle Smallwood Williams, our organization split. During the break of our organization, all national officers changed. That was a golden opportunity for a lot of qualified men and women. It opened the door for bringing forth the talents and capabilities of many people, including my husband and myself. I was not a national president, but I served as a vice-president and chairperson. I was Chair Lady of the International Scholarship Fund for about eight years. I coordinated the giving of scholarships to many of our college-bound students. Many of those same student recipients often tell me thanks for helping them attain their successes and how they're doing in life. I am so proud of them.

In 2008, Apostle Nelson and I were both elected to national office. He was elected to the office of First-Vice Presider of the renamed International Bible Way Church of Jesus Christ, Inc., and I was elected as President of the International Clergy Wives and Widow's Association.

This was quite an honor for both of us. He was the First Vice Presider of one of the largest organizations in Pentecost. This is a position recognized by all reformations and honored and respected by them. I was head of a group of First Ladies, leaders, intelligent, and well-known ladies because of their husbands and accomplishments. We were both humbled and grateful to have been chosen by God first, then selected by our peers and given the honor of serving in these capacities.

He served faithfully for a two-year term of four years, eight years in all. He did whatever he was asked to do. He preached, traveled, planted churches, and lifted the arms of the Presider.

When his tenure was coming to an end, he was nominated for the office of Presider. I thought, Presider? What? Are you kidding me? What? Are you crazy?

I knew he deserved it, he was qualified for it, and I knew he was capable. And I also knew that his nomination was the protocol, but I didn't know if it was possible. I didn't know if it was possible for several reasons.

I wondered if the brethren would vote him into office. His opponent had once served as the Chief Apostle for two terms and was now running again. I wondered if he could get enough votes to win over this well-known, established, capable former Presider. I also wondered if he won and became Chief Apostle and Presider, how would I, as his wife, know how to act and what to do. I wondered many things and wondered, and I wondered.

His opponent was a man with high credentials. He was a man who led the organization well. He was loved, respect-ed, revered, and esteemed highly. Why would anybody attempt to run against such a man? He was a man who was the Pastor of one of the largest churches in the organiza-tion. He led the organization for two prior terms plus during the reorganization period. With his knowledge and experi-ence, why would anyone attempt to run against him?

My husband was not a jealous man, nor was he afraid of anyone's capabilities. He was his own person and confident about this assignment. And, he had received a mandate from God and reassurance that this was his time. He held to his conviction and forged ahead, confident that it was his time and turn. The election day finally came in a St. Louis, MO, Marriott Hotel on March 8, 2014. Apostle Nelson didn't show one bit of nervousness, but I was very nervous, although I tried not to show it. Only the Bishops were al-lowed to vote, so we had to wait patiently for the outcome. Because the election was held in St. Louis, it signified great meaning to me. It was where I lived at one time. It was where I got saved, went to college, graduated from nursing school, was hired on my first real job, was baptized in Jesus' name, received the Holy Ghost, met and married my husband, and had my babies. St. Louis has a lot of history for us. During the convention, many of our former acquaintances, friends, and colleagues in ministry came by to be with us in service. It was beautiful to see them all, and they all said they were pulling for their longtime friend to win the election. I believe they wanted the preacher from the hometown to shine where he started his ministry.

Rumors began to fly but were unfounded. Because he was running unopposed, another candidate was selected to run against him. It didn't work.

My Armor Bearer, a dear friend and very attuned to my needs, was kind enough to wait in my room with me during the election. Since our elevations and elections started, she served me as an Armor Bearer. It seemed like an eternity as we waited. No word came. We waited and waited. No phone call was received. All we could do was wait. I couldn't take it any longer. I texted my husband's Armor Bearer, waiting outside the board room. Still no hint of what was going on; he had heard nothing. I was on pins and needles, waiting for a word on how the vote was going.

As I write this, I can imagine how our President, Barrack Obama, and Michelle felt when he and his family were waiting for the Presidential election results. I can only imagine how a person on trial feels as they nervously await the verdict from the jury to determine his fate.

After about two and a half hours of voting and waiting, I

finally got the text from Apostle Nelson, which said, "I'm the Man." I could tell by his wording that he was as surprised as I was. I screamed with relief. The wait was over. He would be our organization's next Chief Apostle and Presider, the International Bible Way Church of Jesus Christ, Incorporated.

My Armor Bearer wanted to know what was happening and why I was screaming. When I told her that he was the winner, she screamed. God had given us His favor, and He had exalted us in a way that we knew it was Him who did it. We were blessed beyond our dreams. Who knew we would be in this place, with this honor and title, Chief Apostle and Presider and the Elect Lady? Oh my God, I was so humbled. Later, I was told that the ballots were counted more than once. With each counting, Apostle Nelson's name came out on top. All previous Bishops with the title of Presider were born in Bible Way. No one else elected to this office has come from another reformation. He was not Bible Way born, nor did he grow up in a Bible Way church. He came to Bible Way after serving and being ordained in other organizations. Apostle Floyd E. Nelson, Sr., my husband, was the first and only Bishop with God's honor and favored to claim this victory. There may be others to follow, but he was the first.

My immediate thoughts were that I must have a posture of humility. I knew that I must not flaunt myself with arrogance and superiority. I knew I must keep the same respect and honor for my Presider husband. However, I did not feel like the organization's 'First Lady' (Elect Lady). I still felt like my same ole self.

It was hard for me to walk in that role as 'Elect Lady.' After all, I am the young girl from Kansas City who wore old shoes for many days because I wasn't ready to throw them away. I had safety pins in places to hold things together in my youth because I didn't know how to sew. I am the same person who dreamed of being a nurse and a teacher, and God granted my request and much more. I am the same young lady who wanted to marry a Pastor, a Man of God. But there I was, at that juncture in my life, with my Pastor husband that I daydreamed about in my youth, who was now elected as Chief Apostle.

It was hard to fathom.

Neither of us prayed for this to happen. Our prayer was that the will of the Lord be done during the election. I can truthfully say it was the Lord's doing and marvelous in our eyes. We had been elevated, promoted, and revered by our peers. I included myself in this process because my husband and I were one. We were one in marriage and one in spirit. What he did affected me, and what I did affected him. When he won, I claimed myself a winner too. If he did not win, I was right there along with him. One thing was for sure when you saw him; you saw me—Vice versa. If either of our presence was excluded, it was by reason of gender.

Post-election, I was still basking in the joys of victory. We immediately attended the annual Bishop's and wife's dinner. We rode in the limousine with my husband's opponent, his wife, and the newly elected First-Vice Presider. I did not know how this ride to the venue would be because the election was still fresh. Would it be solemn, hostile, silent, or rude? Or would the ride be celebratory? To my surprise, he and his wife were happy for us, congratulated us, and we had an enjoyable evening. Being the distinguished couple they are, I should have expected this reaction. A happy occasion that could have gone sour was squashed because of the integrity of these two men and their wives.

Like wildfire, the word was out. Congratulations came in from around the world. Calls came from England, Africa, Jamaica, Trinidad, and other parts of the globe. The internet is a great resource, and it was used to get the news out, along with videos of the evening service. All I could say was "Thank You, Jesus," for blessing us with such a great blessing and such a high honor. We cannot praise you enough."

Humility is a virtue that is lacking in many people who are in prominent positions. Many of these famous people portray the opposite characteristic of humility. If you want to be great, be a humble individual wherever you are in life. I desired then and now to be used by God. To be a blessing to his people, there is no room for high-mindedness.

Yes, I could boast about many things, brag, and be puffed up because of who men say I am. But I choose to walk humbly before God so He can exalt me. On a day-to-day basis, I didn't feel like the 'Elect Lady,' I felt like the blessed woman I am. I felt like the grateful woman that I am. I knew God had blessed us, and I was thankful and humbled.

My response then is the same as now, "To God be the Glory for the things He has done!"

[8]

From Apostle to Chief

THE DAY OF HIS INSTALLATION WAS HERE. It was a beautiful bright sunny day. We walked outside to the restaurant to eat lunch and saw people congratulating us and wishing us well. God is good. I was still basking at the moment. The euphoria that I was feeling was unbelievable. I felt so blessed. Family, friends, and acquaintances worldwide witnessed the occasion and wished us well. I still couldn't believe this was happening. I had butterflies in my stomach, along with other indications of nervousness. For days leading up to this day, I wondered what I would wear. I wanted to look appropriate for the occasion. I searched high and low for the perfect outfit. I was contacted by a man who could make me the ideal suit to wear, one of a kind. When I visited his shop and saw what was possible for me to wear, I knew. It was beautiful but costly and suitable for a queen. I had seen his work's quality and inspected it with my critical eye, and I decided to use this skillful designer to make my garment. I went over the sample garment entirely, and it met my specification. We made the deal, took measurements, gave him my deposit, and was promised delivery a week or two before we were to leave. That didn't happen.

I waited and waited to receive my tailor-made, one-of-a-kind suit. I didn't want it to arrive at the last minute. Finally, the package arrived the day before we were to leave. After opening the box with anticipation, I immediately knew something was off. I tried it on, zipped it up, and it was too big and didn't fit or look well. To say that I was devastated is an understatement. The quantity and quality of the garment were inferior to the designer quality I had been promised, and I was crushed. What was I going to do? What was I going to wear? It seemed like a last-minute rush job. There was no time for me to shop; we were leaving for the convention the next day.

Not only did I need an appropriate dress, but I also needed a hat and shoes. Hats in the DMV can be costly, but the Apostle didn't mind. He wanted me to have the best, and the price didn't matter. That's the kind of man he was. Nothing was too good or costly for me, and he often told me that. But I always tried to stay on budget and get things on sale at marked-down prices. I refused to pay the regular price for items when one could be economical and have quality. Without being cheap, I would always try to guard our finances and make our money stretch. Quality is of the utmost importance to me, and sometimes you must pay more to get excellence. Thank God I had already purchased my hat and shoes. Fortunately, I had other things in my closet that I could choose from. The suit I decided on was the one I was to wear to our Tuesday night service. It was beautiful and elegant enough for me to wear as my husband became our Chief Apostle. I wanted to make him proud and not embarrassed by how I looked. At the Inauguration Service, thousands of people were there. The ballroom was packed to capacity.

Previously, I was asked to participate in the consecration ceremony by placing the ring on his finger while my husband was installed. The weight of his ring laid heavy in my hand. Finally, I was called to the altar. As I placed the beautiful Apostle's ring on his finger, I could not help but thank God for where he brought us from and where he was taking us. I couldn't help but think that this was the Lord's doing, and it was marvelous in our eyes.

While I walked in this new role, I was given a book a dear friend wrote during the Inaugural Reception. It reminded me that I was a Leading Lady amid my fears, anxieties, and misgivings. It was a book about Queen Ester. In the book, it was stated that we are Queens.

The book says that sometimes before we open our mouths to speak or make a statement on any level, we should feel for the crown on our head. Let the knowledge of wearing a crown cause you to guard the door of your lips and remind you that you have the power and authority to handle any situation. And that you can do all things through Christ who strengthens you. People will make assumptions about you and expect you to show up in fancy, expensive clothes from fancy stores, hair coifed, nails manicured, designer purses, makeup expertly done, and stiletto Red Bottom shoes on your feet. Let none of this move you. Be "the you" God called you to be. In time, they will look beyond your outer appearance and their expectations of you to see the gem within. They will see you show up in the face of pain and adversity, wearing your crown. Smile when you should be crying. Hold your head high when you feel like you are rejected and ignored. Many will notice you trusting God to see you and your husband through all circumstances. Showing up with a meek and quiet spirit is the hidden you, and in the sight of God, a great price. Let them see the crown coupled with grace and humility on your head. Wear the crown proudly. The crown is sacred. The crown is honorable. The crown represents royalty. Always check to see if your crown is on your head straight. Before putting it on your head, make sure you have polished it well with love, kindness, blessings, and humility.

I was given the title "Queen Mother" during this time. I was hesitant to accept this honor because I thought it spoke of piety, exclusivity, and snobbishness. Eventually, after listening to my husband and thoughtful prayer, I received the title and wore it with grace. Queen Mother means that you are the fairest of the fair and the Queen Mother to them all. I would realize that the title was an honor and an identification of love and respect. I was deeply humbled to be called "Queen Mother."

The consecration was now over, and we had a new leader, Chief Apostle Floyd E. Nelson, Sr. He had been consecrated the Fifth Chief Apostle of the International Bible Way Church of Jesus Christ, Incorporated.

An Apostle is the title of the highest ecclesiastical official in the Pentecostal church.

An "Apostle" has a call to plant and oversee churches and has verifiable church plants and spiritual sons and daughters in the ministry. Apostle Nelson had many sons and daughters in the ministry. It was his pleasure to be called dad. He embraced these men and women and encouraged them to be the best and go the distance in their ministry. He was honored and given a beautiful gift entitled "Apostolic Father," which depicted the characteristics of the person with this title. An Apostolic Father described him to a Tee. That's what he tried to be, and that is who he was.

Being an Apostle is a high office and a place of significance. He was a servant who realized he had a debt to pay. Because God had done so much for him and given him a message, so he had to declare it to the nations. He had a unique purpose. He was recognized by other reformations of like faith around the world. Apostle Nelson had the divine calling of an Apostle long before he was consecrated. His works spoke for him. We lost count of how many churches he established, but the number far exceeded one or two.

There have been many years of sacrifice and putting the church first. It was not always easy, and I admit, at first, there was a little resentment on my part. When people mistreated and took advantage of him, he was a 'turn the other cheek' kind of guy. On the other hand, I wanted to defend him because he wouldn't say or do anything to protect himself. If I can be honest, before I was fully saved in my young years, I allowed myself to look at people thinking that they stood in my way from being content with just me and my husband. Oh my, was I wrong! When I began to love the people God had placed in our care, I found absolute joy working with my preacher husband. I realized that the church is designed as a family unit, with the pastor as a father and his wife as the mother. All the parishioners are the offspring. Some are born in the ministry, and some are transplanted from other churches. Whatever the case, we are family.

God is faithful to His word, and we have been immensely blessed. Shortly after we relocated to the East Coast, we looked for a home to rent. We were living in a two-bedroom apartment. The apartment was lovely, but we needed more space.

We knew a young couple from another ministry who offered us his nearly brand-new home. The blessing overtook us while we were guests at another church where Apostle was a guest speaker, and we were about to leave.

A young minister and his wife had tracked us down and came looking for us. The couple told us to follow them. We drove, not knowing where we were going. Finally, we parked in the driveway of a beautiful house. The Apostle said, "Our car would look good parked in this driveway."

We laughed, went inside, looked around, liked what we saw, and were told the house was ours. Miracle after miracle, the Lord did for us.

They were selling the house, and we were looking for a place; it was a perfect match. It was a beautiful two-story home with a full basement, sunken family room, wood-burning fireplace, large kitchen with a center island, and more. I couldn't believe my eyes. All we had to do was move in after signing the necessary papers, and we did. It was beautiful, comfortable, and had four bedrooms (we added the fifth) and two and a half bathrooms. I decorated that house and made it home. It was so big and so spacious, we had room for everything. That was a blessing from God.

I recall another great blessing. We were having car trouble, and our car stopped running at a restaurant. Thank God we were only about a mile from home, and the Apostle walked home to get the other vehicle. The next day, while getting the car repaired, he received a phone call, and the gentleman, a young minister whom we had pastored, told him that the vehicle was parked in our driveway. The keys and the title were in the car. We were gifted a nearly new Mercedes Benz with a free and clear title.

This gifted car was newer than the one we were driving. He didn't sell it to us, he didn't lease it to us, and we didn't have to make a single payment to him. He gave it to us. Unbelievable! Yes, we needed a new car, we wanted a new car, but we were not ready to get one. God saw our needs, and he supplied our needs.

God gave us houses and cars; He also gave us church buildings at ridiculous prices.

There are many more miraculous blessings that God has given us. I know it was our faithfulness, dedication to the ministry, and liberality in giving. Apostle Nelson was a generous giver. I often thought that we couldn't afford to give what he gave. When offerings were given at the church during services, he always gave what they asked for., even in the hundreds of dollars. He was among the first to give at special and sacrificial offering times. Giving was his pleasure. It didn't matter if his name was called, nor did he want to bring attention to himself. We never suffered because of it; there was always more than enough. God is a provider.

After being invited to the island of Nantucket to preach a revival, Nantucket is a resort town populated with rich businesspeople and well-to-do wealthy people, primarily Caucasian. Apostle Nelson saw a great need for a church. The Lord directed him, and he founded another church on the island of Nantucket, Massachusetts. The people there loved him, and there was nothing they wouldn't do for him. They followed him, and in a short time, the church grew. His commitment to Bible Way had increased, so he appointed me as pastor over this church. I wasn't looking for this, but I had a love for the people and accepted the challenge. I did everything from preaching to teaching and special occasion events. I had never pastored before, and some members tried to run over my authority, but the Apostle was with me every step of the way, and that wasn't going to happen. I pastored that church for more than five years. I went back and forth, flying on a nine-seater plane or occasionally taking the ferry. The plane ride was short but scary at times. I would have walked away if I had not been dedicated to the church. After a while, I left that church because of a minor illness that lasted a short time. My Assistant Pastor took over the church's leadership and was left in good hands.

Occasionally, the Apostle and I would sing together; he was a great singer, but only because I knew a bit of music could I carry a tune. However, I once was a lead singer in the choir. Nonetheless, seemingly, he made the song our signature statement.

The title was "I've Decided to Make Jesus My Choice." The words to the song are:

Some folks would rather have houses and lands
Some folks choose silver and gold
But these things they treasure
And forget about their soul
I've decided to make Jesus my choice.
These clothes may be ragged that I'm wearing
Heavy is the load that I'm bearing
These old heavy burdens that I'm carrying
I've decided to make Jesus my choice.
The road is rough, and the going gets tough
And the hills are hard to climb
But I started out a long time ago
And there is no doubt in my mind
I've decided to make Jesus my choice.

In short, because we chose Jesus, God gave us double for our trouble. We were faithful over a few things, and He made us ruler over many. The times we sacrificed taught me to be grateful. It has been a life of one victory after another, and the steps in-between to achieving those victories are memorable. Had I not gone through and climbed those steps, I would not have learned the things I know today. Never despise the day of small things or how you may have to travel.

The road may be taking you to your victory and your destiny. Keep your feet on the path and climb the steps to your future. Someone once said, a winner never quits, and a quitter never wins. You are a winner.

[9]

Distraction, Devastation, or Disaster

APOSTLE NELSON IS AN EASY-GOING, EVEN-TEMPERED, ALWAYS SMILING, ALWAYS GLAD TO SEE YOU. A MAN WHO GAVE A GODLY HUG AND A BROTHERLY KISS ON THE CHEEK. He loved people. He was a kind gentleman. He always wanted to know if everybody was good. He always wanted everybody to feel comfortable in his presence and that they were important, no matter who they were or their importance or unimportance.

If you were in the family of God, he saw you like family, and you were destined to get a hug and maybe a kiss on the cheek.

Early in our marriage, I sometimes told my husband that he should have married someone else. I was having difficulty adjusting to this new role. I was used to doing what I wanted to do when I wanted to. He would say no, he shouldn't have married anyone else. He married the one God wanted him to have. I finally agreed with him because I could see the orchestration of God's handiwork in us.

In the beginning, we decided that whenever he had to go out on pastoral business, he would not go alone; I would go with him. I would not go with him if I were ill or for another valid reason that necessitated my attention.

When he got a dependable, committed adjutant, he sometimes fulfilled those duties accompanied by his adjutant.

There were many incidents where a few females tried to make his ministry a disaster. But, he was covered with prayer and by the blood of Jesus.

I never failed to pray for my husband. I kept a prayer on my lips for his anointing, safety and protection, knowledge, health, and strength. I was his eyes and ears. I saw what he didn't see. God has given me the Spirit of Discernment; when needed, it activates itself. When things didn't seem right, I would tell him to be watchful and prayerful. His manly nature didn't want to listen at first. He soon realized I was right and began to listen to me. When things went awry, he always returned later to tell me, "Thank you, I was right." Sometimes when he was busy or heavy laden with church matters, it was the perfect time for the enemy to creep in. Wolves in sheep's clothing are in our churches, waiting for the right time to strike. Pray for your husband.

I realized that there are beautiful women who are unsaved and in the church. Women who are shapely and full-figured, endowed with curves and edges that help make them attractive. This goes with the territory. A few have gotten out of character and 'come on' to him, expecting me to get out of character and confront them. You may ask, was I jealous, or was I outraged? Hmmm, wellll, maybe only because they ignored my presence and didn't greet me or say a simple hello. I had to tell them I was present and accounted for, so don't try anything stupid. Hello.

One lady, who had visited our church a few times, made a frantic phone call to our home. She said she was seriously ill and needed prayer and couldn't wait until morning.

This lady lived a long way from where we lived, in another state. It had been a long day, and Floyd didn't feel like going to pray for anyone. But he decided to go and insisted that I go with him.

I went along on what felt like an out-of-town journey.

When we arrived at her home, she was outside twirling with a hula hoop in front of her house. She didn't see us right away. She was concentrating on doing the hula for the Bishop. When she noticed that he was there and I was with him, she immediately was healed and got well. Amazing.

This same lady had another "emergency" prayer request and wanted my husband to come to pray for her. When we got there and knocked on the door, she greeted us in a see-through skimpy short 'baby doll' gown. I was standing behind the Apostle, and when she saw me, she was shocked.

She quickly shut the door and said, "wait a minute, I have to go and put some clothes on." Didn't you know you didn't have any clothes on when you opened the door?" Or was she trying to entice the Bishop? Was she hoping that he would be alone? Probably.

My presence thwarted her attempts both times. I confess that there were times that I genuinely did not want to go with him. Maybe I wasn't feeling well or just wanted to chill out and enjoy a quiet evening at home. But I went anyway, regardless of how I felt. It was not that I didn't trust my husband; I did. But I didn't trust the devil. Women will try all types of things to get at your husband. They are very cunning and crafty. They are scheming while we are dreaming and trying while we're crying.

Please be aware that the women in *your* company may also be up to no good, not all of them but some. Please don't expose yourself to just any woman because they are women.

Be watchful and be prayerful.

There was a lady who claimed to be highly anointed in ministry. She came to the church, telling the pastor Bishop that the Lord had sent her to help. She tried several times to get next to the pastor for any reason. She would conjure up reasons to be in his company. She even invited herself to ride along with us to special events.

She was in his Sunday school new members class, but at the time, I was not. The Lord spoke to me and told me that I should start going to his class instead of the women's class. I was a few minutes late the first time I went, and Bishop had already started teaching. When I opened the door to his classroom, she was sitting in the front row right in front of him with her legs spread open and her dress pulled up above her knees. She wanted him to see her. She wanted him to see everything.

Regardless of how anointed a person is, you're still human.

He was so glad when I entered the room, and as soon as I came in, she scrambled to pull her dress down because she knew it was wrong of her to be sitting like that. It was obvious she wanted him, but he didn't want her. This particular lady did not care for me too much. She could not do what she would have liked to do when I came around. My discernment was on high alert, and I picked up her spirit immediately.

Then there's the story of the lady evangelist who told me I shouldn't get married to Floyd. If you remember, I discussed this in a previous chapter. Although, at one time, she was married to a Bishop, and they had a church that was doing well. However, when her husband, the Bishop, got invited to preach at another church or on special occasions, she was always too tired to go or had something else to do. She would ask the secretary to go in her place and represent her. She did this repeatedly so often that she put the secretary right into her husband's arms. I don't think she knew what she was doing at the time. And unfortunately, when she came to her senses and saw what was happening- it was too late. They eventually became a couple. They got married, and the secretary became the First Lady.

Much later, I met that secretary. She was also working in the hospital in the same position that I was working as a surgical nurse. She was a lovely lady, helpful, and cordial to me. She had a very unusual last name, which I noticed right away. I had only known one other person with the same name as hers, the lady from my former church. I asked her about it, and if they were related, she told me the story of how she got her last name. She said her husband's first wife gave him to me. She repeated it and said, "my husband's first wife gave him to me."

Ladies, don't give your husband away as she did. Please don't be too tired to go places with him. Don't be too exhausted to show up. He needs your companionship. He needs to see you in the congregation smiling at him and saying amen. He needs to know that you are there for him. Don't be naïve; somebody wants your husband just like you do. They would like to take your place and be Mrs. so and so. It doesn't matter how fat your husband is, how short he is, how bad his teeth are or how bald his head is. Some women are just plain trifling. They think that because their curves and edges are so voluptuous, they can entice any man, and they will give it a try.

The days of the hula hoop may be over, but women have all kinds of tricks in their bags. They may pull out one of those tricks to try and put a wedge between you and your husband at any given time. Keep your husband covered in prayer so he won't be deceived or enticed by Satan's devices. Words are flattering and cheap, so may I suggest you tell him and show him how valuable he is.

To be clear, somebody wants him, but he married you. He married you for a reason. He married you to be by his side. He married you because you are his soul mate, partner, and companion. He doesn't want these other women; he wants you!

This last story is a real heartbreaker.

We had known this pastor for many, many years. He had a thriving church, and people came from far to near to hear him preach. He had a large membership and was well respected in the city.

One Sunday morning, during the service, his angry, devastated, and hurting wife, got up from her seat, walked over to her husband, and did something despicable to him—so humiliating that I can't tell you what she did because it was too astonishing.

But why would she do such a thing? Why would she do it in front of the whole congregation? What was going on?

It was later made public that the husband had been doing something in the church and that it had been going on for months.

Why did he do such a thing that surely ruined his reputation? What motivated him to step outside his comfortable home and family to seek whatever he was seeking?

He found in someone else what was missing at home. Not only was the church devastated, but the home was destroyed. A wife must strive to be what the man needs in the church and the home. Home comes first and should be built up before the church. Why? Because God established the family before he established the church. I believe that the family comes first in the order of preference. But, the family must be flexible enough to allow the Man of God to do ministry as God dictates.

I should also add that not all women are evil. Not all women or up to no good. Not all women are out to get the man of God. Some have a clean heart and are there to help the Pastor and the church. Even to help you! But the few that are there for other purposes are far too many to count.

It's not that they want to get a man because there are far too many other men on the horizon who are willing and available. Single men, men who are attractive, and men who are ambitious. But Satan uses these women for the primary objective-- to destroy the anointing of God on the one appointed to lead the ministry.

If the enemy can kill that man's influence and his anointing, he has the victory over him and the church. It's the anointing that the enemy wants to destroy because he knows that it's the anointing that makes the difference in your ministry. It's the anointing that removes the burdens, destroys the yokes of bondage, and breaks every chain in the lives of others.

However, it's the anointing that is attractive to women.

It puts the pastor in the limelight, and people want to be seen with people in power, men and women alike.

That's one of the main reasons some people take selfies, on their smartphones, with famous people and put them out on social media. They want to be seen with trendy people.

If the devil gets access to the leader, the church will suffer and be razed. It's proven that if you want a thing to die, you must kill the head.

So, it's always best to be aware of things that could go wrong to avoid the many things that will go wrong. In my years of serving in the church, I know of many incidents where churches were destroyed because of infidelity. Infidelity is as old as Delilah or older, but he doesn't want Delilah; he wants you. Apostle Floyd and I talked about these many incidents happening in the church. The incident just mentioned was open knowledge for everyone to see. When an incident is juicy and fit for gossip, it will spread like wildfire.

We were so grateful that we had each other. We knew what could go wrong involving other women, and we were always together. When you saw him, you saw me, and vice versa, or we were somewhere close by.

It's common for certain women to use flattery. They like to tell pastors and ministers how they love to hear them preach, that they preached well, and so on. They love to be seen overcome by the spirit right before the pulpit. When that happens, it draws attention to them. Compliments are good, but you, the wife, should hear these words first and foremost.

Don't let another woman compliment your husband more than you. Always have a flattering word to tell him, and it doesn't have to be just positive words, but it should be truthful and in love. You praise your own house and honor your husband. He's yours; you picked him. Each time I had an opportunity to introduce Apostle Nelson as the guest speaker or the main speaker at our church, it gave me great joy to introduce him. I pulled out every word in my vocabulary to edify God and thank Him for my husband. He would smile and get a little embarrassed when I talked about him because he didn't want the attention. I was not just flattering him; I expressed my heart and how I felt about him. I wanted to let people know they were about to hear from a man who was one of God's chosen vessels. I was sure they would love his preaching and teaching just as much as I did, and I did love his preaching. He made things so plain that a child could understand.

I would intimate his ability to cite scripture from memory. He would quote one scripture after the other from memory as he delivered the word of God. Preaching and teaching was his element. He would reveal the meaning of scripture and have us sitting on the edge of our seats. I knew he was prolific and relevant for his day—a one-of-a-kind. At many different times, I have seen him minister and operate in the five-fold ministry of Apostle, Evangelist, Prophet Pastor, and Teacher so that the church could be equipped. I wanted them to know that he was one of the best, if not the best—the cream of the crop. Most importantly, I expressed myself this way about him so that if anyone possibly had any ideas about getting between us, they could just put them aside because here I am, his wife.
People watched me when he would minister. They wanted to see my reaction. I was asked why It appeared that I enjoyed his preaching and teaching. My answer was because I did. I thoroughly enjoyed the life-changing Word of God coming from his mouth. It put a yes in my spirit, an amen in my mouth, and a smile on my face.

Floyd was somebody special to me.

I tried to carry myself in such a way to make him proud of the lady God chose to be his wife. I always gave him honor and esteemed him with reverence and respect. After all, he was my hero, covering, and best friend. It is equally important that even when he felt he didn't do such a great job because he didn't feel well, I still told him how proud I was of him.

They know when they bombed out and did not do so well. Tell him how much you enjoyed him anyway, and don't fail to support him in front of the congregation. Not only are people looking at you to see your reaction, but your husband needs your support above all others. No matter how many others say amen and shout and sing his praises, he wants to hear it from you.

Wives, let me leave this last thought with you.

I understand about being a little cautious or nervous about the attempts of other women, but the Apostle would always tell me,

"I married you. I'm going home with you. I don't want anyone else."

If you are a wife and these words sound familiar? Let them be of comfort and reassurance, especially when he takes the time to respect you and tell others how proud he is to be your husband.

Floyd did this for me repeatedly. It eased me further into security within our marriage. Before his accolades and acknowledgment of me, he would often quote the words of a song...

"THIS IS A MAN'S WORLD, this is a Man's World, but it

Wouldn't be Nothing, NOTHING, Without a Woman or a Girl."

(I was his girl.) After saying that, he would say, "I brought my girlfriend with me; stand, honey." Then, he continued with his words of love and honor for me. The congregation loved it and would always look at me to see how I responded. Of course, I always smiled with love as I stood up and gave my signature hand wave greeting. This may be a man's world, but ladies have a role and are valuable in the kingdom.

I have seen with my own eyes, and I am aware that some husbands and wives love to display their love for each other in the public arena. Social media is overrun with couples spelling out their affections to make people believe their relationship is all peaches and cream. But, when they get home and the doors are closed, it's a different story. They are not even cordial to each other, much less lovey-dovey. Sometimes, there is disrespect, hatred, impatience, resentment, rudeness, and jealousy. I think it's good for couples to express their love for each other openly and not be ashamed of the one you married. My theory is that we should treat our spouse like the world is watching us. Always insist that what you do in public be equivalent to or better than what you do in private.

It's always good to remember your wedding vows and your promises made at the altar. Recall them often. There will come a day when you recall those words and react accordingly because of your love for each other. I have no regrets because of something I should have done and didn't do. He not only heard it from my mouth, but I tried to show him that I loved him. Love will prevail through and above all things.

Please, don't allow yourself to be distracted; it could cause devastation, leading to disaster if you become distracted.

[10]

A Preacher and Teacher Par Excellence

APOSTLE NELSON WAS CALLED TO PREACH AS A CHILD. Preaching and teaching were in his blood and his bones. He had a Spiritual DNA for the Word of God because many great preachers have come through the Nelson heritage.

From his childhood, he astounded experienced preachers and Bishops. They loved to hear young Floyd preach. As he worked his way up the preaching ladder, he was often called to deliver messages, and he did it like an experienced preacher, although he was still a child.

He didn't need a manuscript to preach; his words were directly from God. He'd jot down some reference points, etc., but he hated using a manuscript.

There are times when his comrades would try to catch him

off guard. They would wait until the last minute to tell him he was the principal speaker. They thought he couldn't do it or would certainly mess up before the congregation. That never happened.

Even if he was asked at the last minute, and after the service had started and it was time to introduce the speaker, young Floyd would preach the people happy. He was always ready. He was prepared to fulfill the Word:

"Preach the Word; be instant in season, out of season; reprove, rebuke, exhort with all longsuffering and doctrine." 2 Timothy 4:2

Someone once said, "Hold onto your hat because Floyd will preach "at the drop of a hat" if you drop it."

He always had a word and was ready to do as it says in the book of 1 Peter 3:15

But sanctify the Lord God in your hearts: and be ready always to give an answer to every man that asketh you a reason of the hope that is in you with meekness and fear:

His Seminary training helped him immensely. He never seemed afraid, nervous, or apprehensive when he had to preach. It didn't bother him even if notable or famous preachers were in the room.

He believed what the scriptures said in 2 Timothy 2:15:

Study to shew thyself approved unto God, a workman that needeth not to be ashamed, rightly dividing the word of truth.

The very first time that Apostle Nelson preached in a Bible Way service was in Florida. We had driven to the convocation from California. We were new to this crowd and strangers to most of them. It was at a 6:00 A.M 'Early Morning Glory' service. He was brand new to the organization and unknown except for a few acquaintances and the Presider. It was the custom to have preaching after the prayer service. Well, it was said that the preacher that brought the message was ill-prepared and did not do the Word justice. The Presider wanted to light a fire and bless the people before dismissal.

Guess who was asked to fill in and light that fire? Right, you are. Apostle Nelson. Without warning and a hint, he was the one to light the fire, and he did. A few of the Bishops had heard him before, but to others, it was their first time. He stood before the people and delivered a message that blew the congregation away. Everyone wondered, who is this man, and where did he come from? All during the day, the word spread about his message. I heard so many accolades and commendations for the rest of the week, and he and I were elated. I didn't go to that early service because we didn't know he would be asked to preach. He preached and set the church on fire. I should have gone, and I wish I had. This was the first of many fiery and inspiring messages in Bible Way.

In his downtime, he would read and study. He knew he was called to carry this Gospel and had a Rhema, God-given

Word in his mouth, but he wanted to learn all he could about the Word.

Many days and nights, he could be seen surrounded by books, a notepad, and the Bible. Floyd was invited to preach revivals, sometimes lasting for weeks.

He was a gifted preacher.

In our early marriage, Floyd wanted to get closer to the Lord. He told me he wanted to shut himself in the church (a tradition done with fasting and prayer). He wanted to get a spiritual gift from God. I agreed—no communication, no visitors, nothing but prayer and Bible reading. We came out from the fast and the shut-in when the week was over, and he looked great. He had been praying all week, seeking God.

He looked a few pounds thinner, but he looked great. He voluntarily told me that the Lord spoke to him during the shut-in and that He had given him a gift. But, it was not the gift he desired; it was the gift of the Word of Knowledge. That was not what he had asked the Lord for. He wanted the gift of healing. Paraphrased, he said, smiling, "I could have been eating all this time. He could have told me this before I shut myself in." He was given the fantastic gift of the "Word of Knowledge," and he often used it.

The Lord used him to prophesy and lay hands on the sick at various times. He was not gifted in these areas but was supernaturally blessed to use them when needed.

People were tremendously blessed because of this gift. Even today, people tell me that what he told them in the spirit has come to pass.

His messages carried significant meaning. They were life-changing. Souls were saved, delivered, and people were healed.

One of his favorite scriptures is recorded in the book of Psalm:

Psalm 27

The words to the song are:

A PSALM OF DAVID.

The LORD is my light and my salvation; whom shall I fear?

The LORD is the strength of my life; of whom shall I be afraid?

When the wicked, even mine enemies and my foes, came upon me to eat up my flesh, they stumbled and fell.

Though an host should encamp against me, my heart shall not fear:

though war should rise against me, in this will I be confident.

One thing have I desired of the LORD, that will I seek after;

that I may dwell in the house of the LORD all the days of my life,

to behold the beauty of the LORD, and to enquire in his temple.

For in the time of trouble he shall hide me in his pavilion: in the secret of his tabernacle shall he hide me;

he shall set me up upon a rock.

And now shall mine head be lifted up above mine enemies round about me: therefore will I offer in his tabernacle sacrifices of joy;

I will sing, yea, I will sing praises unto the LORD.
Hear, O LORD, when I cry with my voice:
have mercy also upon me, and answer me.

When thou saidst, Seek ye my face; my heart said unto thee,

Thy face, LORD, will I seek.
Hide not thy face far from me;
put not thy servant away in anger:
thou hast been my help; leave me not,
neither forsake me, O God of my salvation.
When my father and my mother forsake me,
then the LORD will take me up.

Teach me thy way, O LORD, and lead me in a plain path, because of mine enemies.

Deliver me not over unto the will of mine enemies:

for false witnesses are risen up against me, and such as breathe out cruelty.

I had fainted, unless I had believed
to see the goodness of the LORD in the land of the living.

Wait on the LORD: be of good courage, and he shall strengthen thine heart: wait, I say, on the LORD.

I also recall things that he would often say when he was imparting the Word, such as:

Praise Him!!!
Protocol to all I don't know to call
I thank God for my bride
I've got my girlfriend with me, stand, honey
Let's bury the ax, but not in each other's forehead

O Lord, I thank You

This is a man's world, but it wouldn't be nothing

Without a woman or a girl

My wife and I met and married in 45 days. You

young fellows might want to talk a lesson from Pop.

Kin folks

Let's have church

Opinions are like noses...everybody's got one

I feel a dance coming on

Your Love Gives Me Such a Thrill, But, Your Love Won't pay My Bills; I Need Money (At Offering Time)

The Weapon Will be Formed, but it will not Prosper

(Referring to Isaiah 54:17)

The Apostle had a melodious voice. He had favorite songs that he would sing from time to time. Such as:

There is none like you

He Touched Me

Because He Lives

I love you Jesus, I worship and adore you

What a friend we have in Jesus

The blood that Jesus shed for me

I searched all over couldn't find nobody

I'll Go, I'll Go; If the Lord Needs Somebody...

(The list goes on)

Most of the time, he would pick up on the song that the soloist or the choir just sang. Either way, his voice was melodious and soul-stirring.

His messages always had divine meaning and left a lasting memory. Many people remember the titles of the sermons that he preached over the years.

I wrote down many of the sermon titles because they were so meaningful.

Here are a few:

Show the House to the House

Breaking the Law of Poverty

Doubt and Worry are Enemies of the Faith

Believing Beyond Death

I'm Getting Ready For My Wedding Day

Get the Doubt Out

Shaking Won't Make It

Life Comes Through Death

This is the Law of the House

You Must Hear What God I'd Saying

What Do You Do While Waiting on the Lord

The Law of Sowing and Reaping

From Survival to Success

The Futility of Worry

It's Not the Harvest; It's the Seed

Having Faith is Not Optional

Can You Say Yes When Every-thing

Around You Is Saying No?

To God Be the Glory

Are You Willing to Sacrifice?

You Must Have Faith Beyond Your Delay

Break the Box

Pickled or Preserved

This Is the House That God Built

Don't Help the Devil

Don't Let the Devil Frustrate Your purpose

You Must Have Faith Beyond Your Dilemma

Do You Know How To Use The Keys?

I Shall Bear the Image Of God

The Keys to Authority

You Can Depend On God's Word

What to Do When Satan Attacks

Total Deliverance

Don't Underestimate the Power of The Seed

While I Was Waiting

What to Do When You Don't Know What to Do

Eat It and Die, Give it and Live

The Devil Didn't Do This; God Did

    Contrary Winds

    Disregard the Facts

    Shaking won't Make it; you've Got to Have Life

    Sleeping Preacher on a Sinking Ship

    Rise and Go Forward

    Drop Your Rocks

    Let's Go to the Other Side

    It Doesn't Look Like What It Will Do

    Never Underestimate the Power of a Seed

Don't Help the Devil
Delivered From Darkness Unto Light
 Your Disaster Is Not your Destiny
You Can't Keep a Good Man Down
The Third Anointing
Believing is Not Easy
Trusting God
 Give Him Something to Get Into
 Half Done or Well Done
Are You a Child of God, Or a Son of God?
When You Could, You Wouldn't
 Now You Want to, and You Can't

He preached many other sermons and teachings, far too numerous to remember or name. Preaching and teaching was his life.

And most of his sermons were highlighted with a demonstration as he preached with a visual aid, you might say. His sermons would come to life when people could see them enacted. He was often told that he preached like someone much older and acted much younger. He had incredible strength and unusual stamina.

Unlike some, he didn't go to the gym daily or exercise at home. But he was strong and had muscles. Several times when he was preaching, he asked a young man if he knew how to ride piggyback and if so, Apostle would ask him if he would get on his back as he continued to preach. The young man was reluctant, but the Apostle would insist he got on his back. He did this to demonstrate that no matter how heavy the load gets, Jesus was there to help us bear our burdens. People were amazed at his strength to allow the young man to do this. Then he called up a fully-grown man, big and robust, who thought he would get on his back. Apostle looked at the man; he paused a minute and said, "The Lord said He won't put no more on you than you can bear." The crowd broke out in praise, and he in a dance.

When he was much younger, he loved to run track and could still outrun the young guys after he got older.

While having a physical exam, a doctor once asked him, "why his heart rate was so good and the beat so strong? "Are you an athlete? Do you exercise?" We both smiled and answered, no, he preaches. The doctor said, "I didn't know preaching could make a man's heart rate that good." I looked at the doctor and said, smiling, "you haven't heard him preach."

All of us chuckled after that.

Floyd had God-given abilities, and the more he preached, the more people wanted to hear. The Apostle had vivid memory. His quick recall of the scriptures was phenomenal. He was ready if a person wanted to challenge him in the Word. He knew the Bible, and if someone was brave enough to dispute what he said, he had proved his point by the time they finished the discussion.

When I was in Bible College, a young man wanted to meet my husband. I arranged it and introduced them. The young man tried to trip him up with a few scriptures. God gave him a quick recall, and the young man gave up.

He didn't just talk off the cuff; he had scriptures to verify what he said.

After his election to Chief Apostle, one of his duties was to teach Noon Day Bible Study at the Holy Convocation. The ballroom was packed every time. Once the Apostle was in his element and was on a roll, the scriptures and the words seemed to come out of nowhere.

People got excited whenever the word was out that he was the main speaker because they knew they would hear a Word.

He established a bond with many pastors. He had a standing invitation and an open the door to churches across the country. New York, Washington, D.C., Connecticut, Massachusetts, Maryland, Missouri, Arkansas, Oklahoma, Tennessee, Kansas, Indiana, Texas, New Mexico, Nebraska, California, Illinois, Alabama, North Carolina and South Carolina, Georgia, Arizona, Florida, Pennsylvania, Colorado, Minnesota, Oregon, Ohio, Michigan, Iowa, Utah, Delaware, Nevada, Virginia, West Virginia, Louisiana, North Dakota, New Jersey, Mississippi, Washington, Kentucky, and other states that I may have forgotten about.

There were many other places around the world where the Apostle left his footprints. Canada, South America, Europe, the United Kingdom, Israel, Asia, Jamaica and Trinidad, West Indies, and Africa; I'm sure I have unintentionally left some places from the list, but the list could and would go on.

Most of the time, I was right there with him. I was saying

amen and encouraging him on. Not only did I feel the anointing, but I also thoroughly enjoyed his preaching. It made me feel proud. I tried my best not to allow any disturbances or disagreements to interfere or come between us when he was scheduled to preach. I knew that any distraction, large or small, could interfere with his sermons and the delivery.

He loved his job and was committed to the call. Apostle tried to teach and instill the same commitment in young ministers, the men, and women under his tutelage. He would often tell them, "Stay in your lane," meaning do what you're asked to do when called upon. No more and no less. Don't try to sneak in a sermon if you are not asked to preach. Don't try to tune-up and preach if you are asked to give the invocation or pray. Do what you are called to do, do your best, and sit down.

Shortly before his transition, he did something he had always wanted to do. Something that serves as a legacy for all generations and those affected by his life.

He wrote a book.

The book is based on a Bible study he did for a week. He wanted to leave something of his teachings here on record.

The book is a complete manuscript of his phenomenal ministry.

I'm so thankful that he fulfilled this dream. It was entitled:

"Are You a Child of God, or a Son of God?"

There is a distinct difference.

[11]

Rest, Recreation, and Relaxation

THE APOSTLE AND I FINALLY LEARNED TO TAKE TIME OUT FOR REST, RECREATION, AND RELAXATION. However, he would always find a way to perform his love for the ministry and work during these times. He did not minister while we were away, only when we were on a cruise. He always felt that the church needed him and if we went away, it was only for a few short days. I was always ready to pack a bag or two and get away. Eventually, he learned he could step away from the church and leave the church in good hands. He trained his ministers well to the point where they could take over in his absence. If I can't leave the church, his thoughts were, I haven't done my job well.

He would say, "It's my job to work myself out of a job." We took many favorite trips that are etched in my memory. I remember being in London, England and visiting the "London Eye," which is said to be the largest Ferris Wheel in the world. We went to this monumental and historical tourist attraction with another couple from the U.S., The weather was chilly, and misty rain fell. We had to wait our turn to get on the wheel, so we stayed in the cold mist.

When we finally got on the wheel, I saw no individual seats, but the spaces for the seats were inside the large cubicles. These cubicles were so large they could hold about 25 people. It had long seats that were arranged side-ways and huge windows where you could stand and look out over the city of London.

It allowed you to see the city of London from a Birdseye view. We had never seen the city of London from this vantage point of nearly five hundred feet tall. It was exciting, and I was thrilled to be here enjoying this with my husband. It took us about an hour to complete the full circle on the wheel, but none of it was wasted. We appreciated that sightseeing tour. We moved around our cubicle to view London from every side and every angle. We took pictures of everything. London is different from the U.S, and we got to see it from the top side of the city. The rain, the chill, nor the fog ruined our day. We were together, and that's all that mattered.

Another of our favorite trips was to Africa, the city of Ghana, and Uganda. I don't think I have ever seen so many Black people at one time. These people were dynamic entrepreneurs working with the skills that God gave them. I remember the Apostle and I purchased some beautiful fabric so we could have African outfits. They were gorgeous, elegant pieces hand-made for us. One-of-a-kind styled and created for us.

We met with Kings and Heads of State. We ate unusual food that tasted pretty good. On our first trip to Africa, the last half of our journey, we stayed in the Volta Region, which is very mountainous. The weather was raining. Our hotel room had a balcony. A small lizard entered our room because we had left the balcony door open while being gone all day. When I saw the lizard, I was terrified. The man of God came to my rescue and ushered the intruder out the same way he came in. There was peace on the mountain top.

I noticed in Africa that people will praise the Lord and do their dance as long as the music is going on. They have been trained to rush to their seats when the music stops to get out of the way and not hinder the service. I love to see them do this. Dressed in African clothing, the beat of the Congo drums, and a guitar, we were ready to have church.

While in Uganda, they had church service all night long. I remember they sang a song, and some words were, "Shake that booty that Jesus gave you; Shake that booty for the Lord!" At first, I couldn't believe my ears, but they sang, danced, and did what the song dictated. It was very expressive but enjoyable. Africa is the Mother Land. It is so expansive and impressive and so beautiful. I believe everyone should try to visit the country of Africa at some point in their life. You will not be sorry.

We journeyed to many other places worldwide, like Rome,

Italy. Rome is said to be a city drenched in history and Christianity. There was so much to see, and we tried to see it all. Vatican City, St Peters Basilica, the beautiful Sistine Chapel, the famous Trevor Fountain, the Colosseum, St Peters Square. We even saw where the Apostle Paul was imprisoned and the Circus Maximus, where the saints were martyred.

The Apostle loved history, and history could be found on almost every street corner in Rome.

After visiting Rome, our trip to Jerusalem, the Holy City, was another awe-inspiring trip. We went there with a large group of delegates. At first, Apostle Nelson was a bit leery about going because of the rumored unrest. There had been bombings and threats of bombings and so forth, and he was not sure we should go because of the dangerous threats. But I wanted to go, and eventually, we went after he prayed about it. We arrived in Tel Aviv on a Friday evening. Much to my dismay, my luggage did not come in, and there was no other flight coming in from the U.S. until Monday because of the Sabbath. I had no clothes and no toiletries. But the people in the group were so kind to me. They gave me everything I needed, new things until I could get my luggage, arriving Monday afternoon.

After eating breakfast, the following day, the Sabbath, we were on our way out of the hotel to board the bus to go on tour. I had gone ahead of Apostle Nelson and boarded the bus, but he was nowhere to be found. He and a few other people were not present, and the bus was ready to leave. I insisted that the bus not move until Apostle Nelson was there. After asking around to see if anyone knew his whereabouts, we discovered that he and a few others had been stuck on the elevator between floors. They could not get the elevator fixed because it was the Sabbath day, and no one worked on the Sabbath in Jerusalem. The observance of the Sabbath is sacred and strictly observed. But the staff saw this incident as an emergency and immediately got help to pry the doors open. The Apostle and the others were safe and sound. I was happy to see him.

Some exciting things about that trip were fishing and having lunch on the Sea of Galilee, where the Apostle Peter fished. We did not fish, but the escorts did. That was amazing. They fished, cooked the fish, and we ate the fish. We also visited Biblical sites such as the Wailing Wall, the Dead Sea, the grave where Jesus was laid, the Mount of olives where we had Holy Communion, the Garden of Gethsemane, and the Dome of the Rock. To name a few. Incidentally, Apostle Nelson went swimming in the Dead Sea. That was an amazing experience. No, I did not get in.

 We were surrounded by many people of various nationalities and religious denominations. Some couldn't speak English very well but could manage to hold a conversation. They knew it was something different about Floyd, but they didn't know what it was until he revealed that he had the Holy Spirit. That made the difference. They wanted to be around him all the time.

There were so many sites to see that we could not see everything, but everything we saw was terrific. Everything we did, saw, and went through was humbling and made the Bible come alive. We walked where Jesus walked. We saw where He was born in the little town of Bethlehem and where He lived in Nazareth. We also went inside the tomb where He was buried and rose again with all power in His hands. I recommend this trip to everyone. It will change your life.

The cruises we took were always enjoyable and relaxing. Our last cruise together was a family cruise. Our children and grandchildren, and other extended family were all there. We had a lovely time, but the Apostle occasionally complained of discomfort. He wasn't feeling well and went to bed while some of us went to the game room to play a few games. I excused myself early because I wanted to go and check on the Apostle. He was still in bed and not feeling well, so I gave him a mild pain reliever to help with his discomfort.

The next day, he seemed to be feeling much better, but I insisted he make an appointment with the doctor as soon as we got back home. I made the appointment, and we went to his primary doctor. The doctor recommended he go to a specialist, which we did. The specialist examined him, and he said, I think it's cancer, with a solemn face. He recommended that we go to a specialist in Baltimore. The specialist at the University of Maryland Hospital confirmed the suspicion.

I was devastated.

Apostle Nelson was always in good health. He maintained his regular check-ups and followed the doctor's orders. He was rarely sick apart from the common cold. He was strong and very capable of doing everyday things throughout the day. He could preach and teach for hours and had the stamina of a younger man.

He still needed to do so much in life—many places to go. And people to see.

Lord, we need him here!

A battery of tests was prescribed, and all gave a conclusive cancer diagnosis. I immediately prayed, believing in God, trusting him for healing and deliverance. The Apostle was placed on chemotherapy and radiation, which worked for a while.

The signs and symptoms were gone.

We were so thankful, so pleased; we resumed our everyday lives of preaching, teaching, and traveling. However, as we journeyed, I was constantly thinking of ways to make him more comfortable and better.

When his Chief Apostle duties increased, and we traveled more, he insisted that I didn't have to cook for him every day. After all the years I'd spent in the kitchen planning and cooking meals for the family, he wanted me to take a break. Since there were several restaurants nearby, some with soul food and they were clean and friendly, with good food: that's what we ate.

Many times, I felt guilty because I wanted him to be happy. So, I would defy the rules and make him a good, hot, home-cooked meal. He loved whatever I cooked, especially my sweet potato pies.

My husband resumed his regular role of preaching, teaching, operating in the prophetic, and blessing the people. We attended the Convention for Bible Way in Alexandria, Virginia.

During this Holy Convocation, Apostle Nelson consecrated the first woman Bishop in the history of Bible Way. There was a lot of controversy over his decision to do this, but he knew that this was the will of the Lord, and he obeyed. He didn't allow the opinions of men to stop him from this assignment. A woman Pastor from Washington, DC, was now the first woman to hold the title of Bishop. It was a beautiful sacred, and Spirit-filled ceremony. The people prayed, sang, and rejoiced as hands were laid on this Woman of God in the Name of Jesus.

Apostle Nelson was re-elected as the organization's chief Apostle for a second term. His First Vice was a humble man and a praying man. Oh, happy day!

As I was getting dressed for the service, somehow, my foot tripped over the rug in our bedroom suite. I stumbled, and I fell. I was alone, by myself, and I fell. I fell hard. When I discovered I could still move, I slowly pulled myself up by the bedspread. I could walk, but painfully. I managed to finish getting dressed and made my way to the service with the assistance of my daughter and granddaughter. I could barely walk because of the pain. I managed to walk into the

room with the head Adjutant General by my side. Still ex-
cruciatingly uncomfortable, I managed to get through the
entire service. Amazingly, I was able to sit through the
whole service, standing when appropriate and able to com-
ply with the excitement of the moment. Immediately after
everything was over, I was taken to the hospital, and in the
emergency room, I learned that I landed so hard that I frac-
tured my pelvis in two places. I remained in the hospital for
ten days.

Shortly after, we were scheduled to go to San Diego, our
former hometown. We traveled to California for Christmas
to spend the holiday with our daughter Karen and her family. We obtained the doctor's approval and were good to
go. However, we were to see the doctor upon our return.
Apostle was called to a Bible Way church in Washington DC
during this time to settle some ecclesiastical problems. The
church needed spiritual advice, and as the Chief Apostle of
the organization, it was his duty to step in and preach,
teach, oversee, and give Spiritual advice. He became the
interim Pastor for about three years. When the church was
ready for a new pastor to be installed, our son, Floyd II, was
on the list of potential pastors.
Floyd II was pastoring our former church, Lively Stone Worship Center, in Landover, MD. The name had been changed
to Kingdom Harvest by this time. The church was doing well
with a nice-sized membership but needed a church building. Deep down in our hearts, we wanted this church for
our son, but there was nothing we could do to get him this

position; he had to meet the requirements on his own.

The church did the necessary things to secure a Pastor. Before voting, they had a process, including drug tests, background checks, and ecclesiastical history. He also had to preach a Sunday morning service and teach a Wednesday night Bible study.

Of all the names of the candidates, Floyd Jr. was over the top and thus selected to be the church's Pastor. His application, personality, and experience had surpassed all the other applicants. Of course, we were delighted that our son had obtained a church and became the Pastor of one of the oldest churches in the District of Columbia. This was a church that we worked with, prayed with, preached in, and loved. God did it. Because we were still there serving, we didn't have to leave. We continued there and became church members, and Apostle continued his work as Diocesan Bishop.

God opened this door and allowed this miracle.

On returning home from the holidays in California, we went to his doctor's appointment. The news from the doctor was devastating, unbelievable. The cancer was back. I heard the words I did not want to hear, but I also knew God was a healer. He was put on another regimen of tests and treatments. He lost his hair and his appetite. His strength was weaker. But his spirit was high, and his faith remained strong.

I tried to remember everything I knew about God and hold on to my faith. I went to every appointment and every treatment with him. I spent many nights in the hospital with him. He kept the faith despite the obstacles. I was right there by his side, holding his hand as we sat.

On Valentine's Day 2019, he called the leading officers together to meet at the church. They came along with their wives. Amid lunch, it was then and there that he disclosed his serious illness to them. He wanted to reveal it to them firsthand and not be sidetracked by rumors. His successor was there with his wife, a man with who we had confidence and trust. He gave them a few instructions like a father talking to his children. I could see the sorrow in their eyes and the eyes of their wives. The disbelief and sadness on their faces could not be mistaken. It was a sad day.

Shortly after that, one Sunday morning during the morning service, Bishop Floyd Jr. gave his father the mic and disclosed his illness to the church. Such bravery and courage cannot be explained. I marvel at his heroism in making these declarations. I was there close by to give him strength if needed, but his faith was sufficient.

He preached his last sermon at the church one Sunday morning. He still showed strength in his body, and his voice was firm. The sermon was: "When You Could You Wouldn't, Now You Want to, and You Cant." He wanted people to know that he did every time he got to praise the Lord. There would be no looking back wishing because he did it every time he got the opportunity.

The radiation treatments were the hardest. He wanted to stop them, but we prayed, and I encouraged him to stick it out. I wanted the Lord to heal him. I knew that the treatment could only go so far, and the complete healing would come from the Lord. He continued with the treatments, and everyone cheered when he finished and got to ring the treatment completion bell. Everyone cheered, even those visiting other patients.

There were many difficult days ahead. Many more 'uphill' times of pain and agony. But he kept the faith.

I would not allow anybody to talk negatively or use defeated language toward me. I didn't want to hear anything negative to destroy my faith. Not even from the doctor. Looking at it now, I can tell I was in denial. I was in denial of him being sick, and I was in denial at the thought of losing him. I didn't want to hear anything of the sort; I just wanted to keep my faith. Whenever the doctors started to talk, and I felt like it regarded his prognosis, I left the room. Floyd Jr. was there to hear the details. I couldn't take it. I didn't want to listen to the inevitable.

I couldn't take it.

The more I heard and saw, the more it ripped my heart out. It was too much for me to bear alone.

I frequently cried, "Lord, you have to help me."

He began to lose weight because he could only eat certain foods. His appetite was not the best, so I prepared his meals with love and care so we could get the nourishment in his body that he needed.

He never stopped attending church. I sat directly behind him to keep my eye on him. He would praise the Lord in the dance at some point in the service, and I didn't want him to hurt himself.

Caring for him was exhausting, but it was a labor of love. I was drained from the daily routine, but I was there for him, whatever he needed or wanted. He rarely asked for pain medication.

He wanted me to sit by his side at every convenient moment, and I did. We would sit together all day, hand in hand when I wasn't busy.

All-day long, Floyd was smiling. It was a peaceful smile. He smiled when he looked at me, and I smiled back at him. It seemed he couldn't take his off me. In his physical weakness, he remained firm, doing things for himself. He was determined not to allow me to do everything he could do. He was still looking out for me. I thought of different things that I could do to make him more comfortable and less painful. I did those things and saw that he was as comfortable as possible. It made him feel better, and it made me more grateful.

There are five stages when facing death.

Denial, Anger, Bargaining, Depression, and Acceptance. I'm sure I went through them all. Even though I was not the patient, I felt what he felt.

After a long day, and all the chores were done, I stood by the bed where he was sitting up, right beside Floyd Jr. He pulled me close to him and thanked me for the years of our lives together. He told me that I was a good wife. He told me other things and how much he loved me. He also said to me about the plans for my future.

It was our custom to pray together each night before going to bed. We prayed together that night for the last time. I had no idea this would be the last time we would talk to each other, but he knew. I lay beside him, got as close to him as possible, and laid my hand on his chest to reassure him that I was there. I went into a deep sleep.

I didn't know it was coming so soon.

The sound of the alarm from the ventilator pried me out of my sleep.

He had slipped away.

My husband, my friend, and my companion was gone.

The Lord came into the room, called his name, and peacefully took him to be with him.

The Bible tells us in 2 Corinthians 5:8:

We are confident, I say, and willing rather be absent from the body and to be present with the Lord.

I have learned from my husband's teaching that God can heal a person in three ways:

He can instantaneously remove the disease or discomfort

He can heal you gradually

He can take you out of the disease.

Either way, God chooses to heal you is healing. The Apostle was indeed healed.

I had to remember that God gave him to me and the world, and he was on an assignment. On a mission, he was a General and Commander in Chief in God's army. And when his work was finished, he placed his sword in the sands of time and was called off the battlefield to study war no more. He fought a good fight, he finished his course, and he kept the faith. The battle is fought, and the victory is won.

Well done, good and faithful servant, well done.

The days and nights following are painful and blurry.

So much took place before I woke up at the Ritz Carlton.

The day of his internment-- April 13, 2019.

What followed that day.... you already know.

I will always be grateful for this man who obeyed the voice of God and selected me to walk with him on this journey. I thank God for the time and years He allowed us to spend together. Despite challenging times, I would not trade my journey for anything. I cherish the lessons I've learned and the wisdom I've gained, which all add to the bottom line: love.

And, if I had the opportunity.... I would do it all over again.

Perhaps this book would not have been written had it not been for the kind persuasion of a dear friend, whose name I will not mention. I am a very private person, and I respect my privacy. Making my life an open book is a difficult thing. After all, who wants to be criticized for telling their story. Not many First Ladies are willing to write their biography for public scrutiny, especially when they are in the public eye and their husband is well known. But, while this writing was painful, this writing helped to bring healing to me. We have nothing to hide. Thank you, my friend, for kindly nudging me and insisting that I get started. I have no regrets; I am not feeling sorry for myself or sad. I have been told I have more work to do and am available. I pray that the things I have written on these pages will be a blessing to someone and encourage and uplift someone on your journey.

To all my family, friends, and colleagues,
I want to tell you that I love you and am grateful for whatever strength you gave me on this journey.
Because yesterday is gone.
Today is almost over.
And tomorrow is not promised.

FINAL TRIBUTE

To my Floyd,

There are no words, no sentences, no paragraphs, no manuscripts or volumes of books that could convey the impact of your leaving me. Although you had many titles and wore many hats—Chief Apostle, Bishop, Pastor, Father, Brother, Mentor, and Friend....to me, you were simply Floyd. Floyd was my rock. You were my everything here on earth. My Friend, my confidant, my provider, my protector, my travel buddy, and my first-class gentleman. You always opened doors for me, held my chair open, and treated me like a lady.

I was very proud to take on the name; Mrs. Floyd Nelson was so pleased to walk by your side and proud to work with you in the many churches. We shared ministry - you made me proud. I was proud, and Karen, Kristina, and Floyd Jr. were exceptionally pleased to call you dad. You were an excellent father and provider for our family.

Our love was put to the ultimate test during the last few months of your sickness. I told you many times that you were my hero, my brave warrior, and what a giant of a man you were. Throughout your illness, I never heard you complain. Even when your body was in unbearable pain and discomfort, you still had a smile and praise. I love you even now. I not only told you but also tried to show you by honoring and serving you. I looked up to you, respected and obeyed you— at least most of the time.

To say that I miss you is an understatement. We were together for more than fifty years. We traveled, ate, shopped, worked, planned, prayed, laughed, cried, and had fun together. Whatever we did…. We did it together.

You were an incredible gift to the body of Christ and impacted so many lives. You were a people person, from the babies to the seniors. People were important to you, and they were drawn to you. Over the years, I learned that I could not be selfish, I had to share this gift with the world, and I did.

Although you were known for your electrifying preaching and teaching and quick recall of the Scriptures by book, chapter, and verse, you made your mark across the world in your dance before the Lord. Most people didn't know that it wasn't just dancing because you knew how to dance or dancing to entertain the people; your praise was genuine and from the heart. You loved the Lord. I tried to get you to teach me…I watched you glide across the floor. I saw others try to imitate you; they watched you close…they thought they had it. You were often imitated but never duplicated.

It took a special anointing to dance like that.

You would have celebrated 75 years of ministry a few months before your transition. You started as a child and dedicated your entire life to the ministry of the Gospel. Floyd, I know you can't hear me, but I want the world to know that you fought a good fight. You finished your course. And you kept the faith. Your faith was so strong in God, and we were looking for the day God would heal you. But the Lord granted you total healing and complete deliverance when He called you home to be with Him. Now is laid up for you a crown of righteousness, which the Lord, the Righteous Judge shall give you that day; and not to you only, but unto all them also that love His appearing.

Continue to Rest in Peace, beloved. I will always love you.

ABOUT THE AUTHOR

Dr. Nelson loves doing ministry to all ages, both men and women. She also enjoys traveling to new countries to meet new people and learn about their cultures.
She loves reading, watching TV documentaries, playing challenging video games, and spending time with her

grandchildren—a student of the bible who's always ready to learn from knowledgeable and relevant teaching. In her spare time, she loves to read and brush up on her knowledge of the medical arts.

Made in the USA
Middletown, DE
02 July 2022

68040659R00076